Contents

Introduction   i
Preface   iv
Snow-Blinded on the Summit   1
Waiting in the Wilderness   13
Winter Mountaineering   27
Trees at Timberline   40
Wind-Rapids on the Heights   50
The Arctic Zone of High Mountains   59
Naturalist Meets Prospector   67
The White Cyclone   75
Lightning and Thunder   81
Landmarks   92
Children of My Trail School   103
A Day with a Nature Guide   121
Play and Pranks of Wild Folk   131
Censored Natural History News   141
Harriet—Little Mountain Climber   151
Evolution of Nature Guiding   161
Development of a Woman Guide   173
Enda by Esther Burnell Mills   186

Dedication
To Elizabeth Frayer Burnell
A Nature Guide

Elizabeth Frayer Burnell with her niece,
Enda Mills.

Adventures of a Nature Guide

Enos A. Mills

With "Enda" by Esther Burnell Mills

Temporal Mechanical Press
Longs Peak, Colorado

Temporal Mechanical Press
a division of Enos Mills Cabin
6760 Hwy 7
Estes Park, CO 80517-6404
www.enosmills.com
info@enosmills.com

ISBN 978-1-928878-41-4

Title page photograph: Enos A. Mills and his daughter, Enda,
looking over Tahosa Valley and Long's Peak. Photograph by
Esther Burnell Mills

Cover photograph by Eryn V. Mills.

Introduction

Growing up, my Daddy would bring out a wonderful letter from my great-grandfather Enos Sr., to his son Enos Jr., my grandfather, where he said, "I do not know if there is a God, I do not know if there is not, but my opinion will not change the facts." Teaching, sharing such an essential component of logic, reinforcing internal freedom of self-delusion. I hold that letter now, and I may touch brittle paper and see fading ink, what I feel is the electricity of wisdom.

This is a exquisite time to be alive. Science confronting supersition, our age of reason requiring logic, our intellectual, physical and metaphysical perspectives of life being revealed. Moments of clarity, that spark of understanding, where you see the world in a glorious distinction, with new wonder of how amazingly luminous the dance of the universe is...and your outlook is never the same.

Learning is about the process of continual brain stretching experiences that prepare us for the challenges life provides. Letting our naked brains take us on adventures, letting go of our human perspective and jumping into the pool of molecular *Jamais vu* as though we have never experienced life on this globe, in this atmosphere. Giving up all the theories disguised as information is the first bounce toward what genuinely is, we shed assumption for discovering, and we experience the flow of reality. Engaging our infinite intellect in stimulating activity that makes it even more adept, is exhilarating.

Brain evolution is authentic for the individual experience. We live in an environment we must adapt to from the day we enter this reality. Inauspicious habits, handed down over the years, from people who supposedly didn't know any better suffering from mental anguish. Behaviors, human operating procedures, perhaps comes down to how we've been taught and knowing the possibilities. At the end of the day we all want to say we did our best.

It appears that we are a sum of what we learn from all our personal encounters. The bland or injurious, or the inspiring and generous of spirit, it is what we actively choose to keep and what we discard from our encounters...from the good or the unpleasant...or the horrible.

As a toddler, I was sexually violated. Abhorrent behavior was taught under the guise of healthy. When my parents found out, everything became inside out, and 50 very odd years of a confusing and terrifying life began. I was then controlled by fear, derision and exclusion, including years of fighting the obligation to commit suicide. That phase ended with letting go of my attachment to another person's version of my story and creating and embracing new neural pathways of logic and facts...and forgiveness.

Imagine a society that collectively chooses to treat all babies as the infinite brains that they are, instead of the exploitable, taking unfair advantage of the vulnerable.

How my brain has changed is what I find extraordinary! The terror, hysteria, confusion, fog, frustration, the feeling of sabotage and most of the time the anger, are gone. Where I used to have uncertainty, I have memories. The mystery that was my life is fading...I'm moving on to the mystery of... what will my life be now? I'm flooded with comprehension, recall is quicker, I wake up having solved a problem during sleep and my creativity has jumped into paradigm shifts. Clarity is an adventurous guide.

The most important choices we make are in choosing and knowing virtuous guides. Individuals that comprehend Enos' thought "the question is the door to a child's mind" and what phenomenal potential lay there, are sought out by exploring brains. We are all travelers, teaching people how to live and adventure...or how not to. It's all about the elements of authentic existence, of experiencing the wonders of being alive, pleasant and unpleasant and learning how to cope with the realities that challenge every life form. We are better when we choose to flow with nature than against it.

Teaching is the oldest and most natural thing we do, just by how we live and behave. When we are appropriately educated we learn the why's, not just the how's. To purposely withhold or incorrectly educate any brain is to create a vacuum that nature abhors...in our own lives. Choosing to examine fractals in our environment with a child is to feel the liberty of exploration. In learning a new viewpoint, we feel a bit more of that connection the universe has for each and every spirit that lives on our lovely planet, being reminded that we are wanted here and now at full brain proficiency.

Consciousness is our daily experience of this wonderful existence on planet Earth, perhaps we won't be in this neck of the Milky Way again for awhile. Simply by being glad we're alive, amazed, exhilarated about the sensation of everything. May we all have a splendid look at the fascinating in our everyday adventures.

Elizabeth
Long's Peak, Colorado

People like you and I, though mortal of course, like everyone else, do not grow old no matter how long we live. What I mean is that we never cease to stand like curious children before the great Mystery into which we were born.
Albert Einstein

Esther Burnell Mills and her daughter, Enda Mills, at Long's Peak Inn.

Preface

The individual interested in the world of outdoors, in many-sided natural history, finds entertainment everywhere in the wilderness, through all the seasons. Storm, sunshine, night, desert, stream, and forest are crowded with waiting attractions and moving scenes.

To have the most adventures and the greatest enjoyment in a given time, ramble the wilds alone and without a fishing rod or a gun. The rambler is free to wander afar and to enjoy the multitude of adventures that come thick and fast upon him. The wilderness being the safety zone of the world these experiences are likely to be less dangerous than staying at home. The hunter, however, armed and killing, multiplies dangers, and in giving his attention to game wanders but little and enjoys less variety and fewer adventures.

The chapters in this book are filled with the experiences and adventures which came to me as a solitary and unarmed camper in the wilds of the continent. These and other experiences, together with inheritances not so tangible, produced definite results; I became a mountain climber and a peak guide. In doing this I developed nature guiding, that is, helping people to become happily acquainted with the life and wonders of wild nature.

The people of the United States have within the past generation created national parks, state parks, city parks, and made wildlife reservations, recognizing their higher values to people, for their uses in education, recreation, and hopefulness. I wish that every park had a nature guide and that every wild place might early become a park.

There now are a number of Cabinet positions, each with a secretary to control and direct its work. But is it not time to have a Director of Parks and Recreation, something for all time and for all people? Instead of one man directing this there should be a number, a board of directors, who are directly responsible to the public. This should be a department separate from and independent of all Cabinet positions and should outrank them.

A number of these chapters were written especially for this book. I appreciate the courtesy of the editors in allowing me to reproduce the articles which appeared in the following magazines: "Snow-Blinded on the Summit" and "Trees at Timberline" in *Country Life;* "Waiting in the Wilderness", "Censored Natural History News", "Winter Mountaineering", "Children of My Trail School", and "Lightning and Thunder" in *The Saturday Evening Post;* "A Day With a Nature Guide" in *The Outlook;* "Play and Pranks of Wild Folk" and "Naturalist Meets Prospector" in *The American Boy;* "The White Cyclone" in *Outing;* and "Wind Rapids on the Heights" in *Harper's.*

Enos A. Mills, Long's Peak

Enos A. Mills, with his daughter, Enda, on his back, guiding a group near Long's Peak.

Let the moulders of public opinion in the chief subjects usually called humanistic—history, sociology, economics, politics, ethics, religion—once they come to see how fundamentally soundness of view and healthfulness of life in all these domains are dependent upon correct elementary information about nature, and innumerable students of educational problems, teachers, and public-spirited and philanthropic persons concentrate their thought and ingenuity upon surmounting the practical difficulties in the way of securing the contact with nature which is indispensable to such information and attitude.

—Dr. William E. Ritter.

Snow-Blinded on the Summit

As I climbed up out of the dwarfed woods at timberline in the Rocky Mountains and started across the treeless white summit, the terrific sun glare on the snow warned me of the danger of snow-blindness. I had lost my snow glasses. The wild attractions of the heights caused me to forget the care of my eyes and I lingered to look down into canyons and to examine magnificent snow cornices. A number of mountain sheep also interested me. Then for half an hour I circled a confiding flock of ptarmigan and took picture after picture.

Through the clear air the sunlight poured with burning intensity. I was 12,000 feet above the sea. Around me there was not a dark crag nor even a tree to absorb the excess of light. A wilderness of high, rugged peaks stood about—splendid sunlit mountains of snow. To east and west they faced winter's noonday sun with great shadow mantles flowing from their shoulders.

As I started to hurry on across the pass I began to experience the scorching pains that go with seared, sunburnt eyes—snow-blindness. Unfortunately, I had failed to take even the precaution of blackening my face, which would have dulled the glare. At the summit my eyes became so painful that I could endure the light only a few seconds at a time. Occasionally I sat down and closed them for a minute or two. Finally, while doing this, the lids adhered to the balls and the eyes swelled so that I could not open them.

Blind on the summit of the Continental Divide! I made a grab for my useful staff which I had left standing beside me in the snow. In the fraction of a second that elapsed between thinking of the staff and finding it my brain woke up to the seriousness of the situation. To the nearest trees it was more than a mile, and the nearest house was many miles away across ridges of rough mountains. I had matches and a hatchet, but no provisions. Still, while well aware of my peril, I was only moderately excited, feeling no terror. Less startling incidents have shocked me more, narrow escapes from street automobiles have terrified me.

It had been a wondrous morning. The day cleared after a heavy fall of fluffy snow. I had snowshoed up the slope through a ragged, snow-carpeted spruce forest, whose shadows wrought splendid black-and-white effects upon the shining floor. There were thousands of towering, slender spruces, each brilliantly laden with snow flowers, standing soft, white, and motionless in the sunlight. While I was looking at one of these artistically decorated trees, a mass of snow dropped upon me from its top, throwing me headlong and causing me to lose my precious eye-protecting snow glasses. But now I was blind.

With staff in hand, I stood for a minute or two planning the best manner to get along without eyes. My faculties were intensely awake. Serious situations in the wilds had more than once before this stimulated them to do their best. Temporary blindness is a good stimulus for the imagination and the memory—in fact, is good educational training for all the senses. However perilous my predicament during a mountain trip, the possibility of a fatal ending never even occurred to me. Looking back now, I cannot but wonder at my matter-of-fact attitude concerning the perils in which that snow-blindness placed me.

I had planned to cross the pass and descend into a trail at timberline. The appearance of the slope down which I was to travel was distinctly in my mind from my impressions just before darkness settled over me.

Off I slowly started. I guided myself with information from feet and staff, feeling my way with the staff so as not to step off a cliff or walk overboard into a canyon. In imagination I pictured

Enos A. Mills on the Continental Divide.

myself following the shadow of a staff-bearing and slouch-hatted form. Did mountain sheep, curious and slightly suspicious, linger on crags to watch my slow and hesitating advance? Across the snow did the shadow of a soaring eagle coast and circle?

I must have wandered far from the direct course to timberline. Again and again I swung my staff to right and left hoping to strike a tree. I had traveled more than twice as long as it should have taken to reach timberline before I stood face to face with a low-growing tree that bristled up through the deep snow. But had I come out at the point for which I aimed—at the trail? This was the vital question.

The deep snow buried all trail blazes. Making my way from tree to tree I thrust an arm deep into the snow and felt of the bark, searching for a trail blaze. At last I found a blaze and going on a few steps I dug down again in the snow and examined a tree which I felt should mark the trail. This, too, was blazed.

Feeling certain that I was on the trail I went down the mountain through the forest for some minutes without searching for another blaze. When I did examine a number of trees not another blaze could I find. The topography since entering the forest and the size and the character of the trees were such that I felt I was on familiar ground. But going on a few steps I came out on the edge of an unknown rocky cliff. I was now lost as well as blind.

During the hours I had wandered in reaching timberline I had had a vague feeling that I might be traveling in a circle, and might return to trees on the western slope of the Divide up which I had climbed. When I walked out on the edge of the cliff the feeling that I had doubled to the western slope became insistent. If true, this was most serious. To reach the nearest house on the west side of the range would be extremely difficult, even though I should discover just where I was. I believed I was somewhere on the eastern slope.

I tried to figure out the course I had taken. Had I, in descending from the heights, gone too far to the right or to the left? Though fairly well acquainted with the country along this timberline, I was unable to recall a rocky cliff at this point. My staff found no bottom and warned me that I was at a jumping-off place.

Increasing coolness indicated that night was upon me. Darkness did not matter, my light had failed at noon. Going back along my trail a short distance I avoided the cliff and started on through the night down a rocky, forested, and snow-covered slope. I planned to get into the bottom of a canyon and follow downstream. Every few steps I shouted, hoping to attract the attention of a possible prospector, miner, or woodchopper. No voice answered. The many echoes, however, gave me an idea of the topography—of the mountain ridges and canyons before me. I listened intently after each shout and noticed the direction from which the reply came, its intensity, and the cross echoes, and concluded that I was going down into the head of a deep, forest-walled canyon, and I hoped, traveling eastward.

For points of the compass I appealed to the trees, hoping through my knowledge of woodcraft to orient myself. In the study of tree distribution I had learned that the altitude might often be approximated and the points of the compass determined by noting the characteristic kinds of trees.

Canyons of east and west trend in this locality carried mostly limber pines on the wall that faces south and mostly Engelmann spruce on the wall that faces north. Believing that I was traveling eastward I turned to my right, climbed out of the canyon, and examined a number of trees along the slope. Most of these were Engelmann spruces. The slope probably faced north. Turning about I descended this slope and ascended the opposite one. The trees on this were mostly limber pines. Hurrah! Limber pines are abundant only on southern slopes. With limber pines on my left and Engelmann spruces on my right, I was now satisfied that I was traveling eastward and must be on the eastern side of the range.

To put a final check upon this—for a blind or lost man sometimes manages to do exactly the opposite of what he thinks he is doing—I examined lichen growths on the rocks and moss growths on the trees. In the deep canyon I dug down into the snow and examined the faces of low-lying boulders. With the greatest care I felt the lichen growth on the rocks. These verified the information that I had from the trees—but none too well. Then I felt over the moss growth, both long and short, on the trunks and lower limbs of trees, but this testimony was not absolutely convincing. The moss growth was so nearly even all the way around the trunk that I concluded that the surrounding topography must be such as to admit the light freely from all quarters, and also that the wall or slope on my right must be either a gentle one or else a low one and somewhat broken. I climbed to make sure. In a few minutes I was on a terrace—as I expected. Possibly back on the right lay a basin that might be tributary to this canyon. The reports made by the echoes of my shoutings said that this was true. A few minutes of travel down the canyon and I came to the expected incoming stream, which made its swift presence heard beneath its cover of ice and snow.

A short distance farther down the canyon I examined a number of trees that stood in thick growth on the lower part of what I thought was the southern slope. Here the character of the moss and lichens and their abundant growth on the northerly sides of the trees verified the testimony of the tree distribution and of previous moss and lichen growths. I was satisfied as to the points of the compass. I was on the eastern side of the Continental Divide traveling eastward.

After three or four hours of slow descending I reached the bottom. Steep walls rose on both right and left. The enormous rock masses and the entanglements of fallen and leaning trees made progress difficult. Feeling that if I continued in the bottom of the canyon I might come to a precipitous place down which I would be unable to descend, I tried to walk along one of the side walls, and thus keep above the bottom. But the walls were too steep and I got into trouble.

Out on a narrow, snow-corniced ledge I walked. The snow gave way beneath me and down I went over the ledge. As I struck, feet foremost, one snowshoe sank deeply. I wondered, as I wiggled out, if I had landed on another ledge. I had. Not desiring to have more tumbles, I tried to climb back up on the ledge from which I had fallen, but I could not do it. The ledge was broad and short and there appeared to be no safe way off. As I explored again my staff encountered the top of a dead tree that leaned against the ledge. Breaking a number of dead limbs off I threw them overboard. Listening as they struck the snow below I concluded that it could not be more than thirty feet to the bottom.

I let go my staff and dropped it after the limbs. Then, without taking off snowshoes, I let myself down the limbless trunk. I could hear water running beneath the ice and snow. I recovered my staff and resumed the journey.

In time the canyon widened a little and traveling became easier. I had just paused to give a shout when a rumbling and crashing high up the right-hand slope told me that a snowslide was plunging down. Whether it would land in the canyon before me or behind me or on top of me could not be guessed. The awful smashing and crashing and roar proclaimed it of enormous size and indicated that trees and rocky debris were being swept onward with it. During the few seconds that I stood awaiting my fate, thought after thought raced through my brain as I recorded the ever-varying crashes and thunders of the wild, irresistible slide.

With terrific crash and roar the snowslide swept into the canyon a short distance in front of me. I was knocked down by the outrush or concussion of air and for several minutes was nearly smothered with the whirling, settling snow-dust and rock powder which fell thickly all around. The air cleared and I went on.

I had gone only a dozen steps when I came upon the enormous wreckage brought down by the slide. Snow, earthy matter, rocks, and splintered trees were flung in fierce confusion together. For three or four hundred feet this accumulation filled the canyon from wall to wall and was fifty or sixty feet high. The slide wreckage smashed the ice and dammed the stream. As I started to climb across this snowy debris a shattered place in the ice beneath gave way and dropped me into the water, but my long staff caught and by clinging to it I saved myself from going in above my hips. My snowshoes caught in the shattered ice and while I tried to get my feet free a mass of snow fell upon me and nearly broke my hold. Shaking off the snow I put forth all my strength and finally pulled my feet free of the ice and crawled out upon the debris. This was a close call and at last I was thoroughly, briefly, frightened.

As the wreckage was a mixture of broken trees, stones, and compacted snow I could not use my snowshoes, so I took them off to carry them till over the debris. Once across I planned to pause and build a fire to dry my icy clothes.

With difficulty I worked my way up and across. Much of the snow was compressed almost to ice by the force of contact, and in this icy cement many kinds of wreckage were set in wild disorder. While descending a steep place in this mass, carrying snowshoes under one arm, the footing gave way and I fell. I suffered no injury but lost one of the snowshoes. For an hour or longer I searched, without finding it.

The night was intensely cold and in the search my feet became almost frozen. In order to rub them I was about to take off my shoes when I came upon something warm. It proved to be a dead mountain sheep with one horn smashed off. As I sat with my feet beneath its warm carcass and my hands upon it, I thought how but a few minutes before the animal had been alive on the heights with all its ever wide-awake senses vigilant for its preservation; yet I, wandering blindly, had escaped with my life when the snowslide swept into the canyon. The night was calm, but of zero temperature or lower. It probably was crystal clear. As I sat warming my hands and feet on the proud master of the crags I imagined the bright, clear sky crowded thick with stars. I pictured to myself the dark slope down which the slide had come. It appeared to reach up close to the frosty stars.

The lost snowshoe must be found, wallowing through the deep mountain snow with only one snowshoe would be almost hopeless. I had vainly searched the surface and lower wreckage projections but made one more search. This proved successful. The shoe had slid for a short distance, struck an obstacle, bounced upward over smashed logs, and lay about four feet above the general surface. A few moments more and I was beyond the snow-slide wreckage. Again on snowshoes, staff in hand, I continued feeling my way down the mountain.

My ice-stiffened trousers and chilled limbs were not good traveling companions, and at the first cliff that I encountered I stopped to make a fire. I gathered two or three armfuls of dead limbs, with the aid of my hatchet, and soon had a lively blaze going. But the heat increased the pain in my eyes, so with clothes only partly dried, I went on. Repeatedly through the night I applied snow to my eyes trying to subdue the fiery torment.

From timberline I had traveled downward through a green forest mostly of Engelmann spruce with a scattering of fir and limber pine. I frequently felt of the tree trunks. A short time after leaving my campfire I came to the edge of an extensive region that had been burned over. For more than an hour I traveled through dead standing trees, on many of which only the bark had been burned away; on others the fire had burned more deeply.

Pausing on the way down, I thrust my staff into the snow and leaned against a tree to hold snow against my burning eyes. While I was doing this two owls hooted happily to each other and I listened to their contented calls with satisfaction.

Hearing the pleasant, low call of a chickadee I listened. Apparently he was dreaming and talking in his sleep. The dream must have been a happy one, for every note was cheerful. Realizing that he probably was in an abandoned woodpecker nesting hole, I tapped on the dead tree against which I was leaning. This was followed by a chorus of lively, surprised chirpings, and one, two, three!—then several—chickadees flew out of a hole a few inches above my head. Sorry to have disturbed them, I went on down the slope.

At last I felt the morning sun in my face. With increased light my eyes became extremely painful. For a time I relaxed upon the snow, finding it difficult to believe that I had been traveling all night in complete darkness. While lying here I caught the scent of smoke. There was no mistaking it. It was the smoke of burning aspen, a wood much burned in the cook-stoves of mountain people. Eagerly I rose to find it. I shouted again and again but there was no response. Under favorable conditions, keen nostrils may detect aspen-wood smoke for a distance of two or three miles.

The compensation of this accident was an intense stimulus to my imagination—perhaps our most useful intellectual faculty. My eyes, always keen and swift, had ever supplied me with almost an excess of information. With them suddenly closed my imagination became the guiding faculty. I did creative thinking. With pleasure I restored the views and scenes of the morning before. Anyone seeking to develop the imagination would find a little excursion afield, with eyes voluntarily blindfolded a most telling experience.

Down the mountainside I went, hour after hour. My ears caught the chirp of birds and the fall of icicles which ordinarily I would hardly have heard. My nose was constantly and keenly analyzing the air. With touch and clasp I kept in contact with the trees. Again my nostrils picked up aspen smoke. This time it was much stronger. Perhaps I was near a house! The whirling air currents gave me no clue as to the direction from which the smoke came, and only echoes responded to my call.

All my senses worked willingly in seeking wireless news to substitute for the eyes. My nose readily detected odors and smoke. My ears were more vigilant and more sensitive than usual. My fingers, too, were responsive from the instant that my eyes failed. Delightfully eager they were, as I felt the snow-buried trees, hoping with touch to discover possible trail blazes. My feet also were quickly, steadily alert to translate the topography.

Occasionally a cloud shadow passed over. In imagination I often pictured the appearance of these clouds against the blue sky

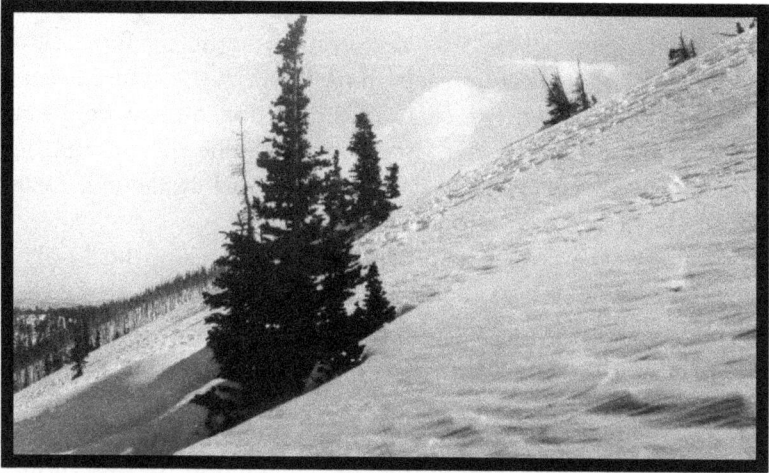

Climbing Snowy Steps on Battle Mountain,
Rocky Mountain National Park.

and tried to estimate the size of each by the number of seconds its shadow took to drift across me.

Mid-afternoon, or later, my nose suddenly detected the odor of an ancient corral. This was a sign of civilization. A few minutes later my staff came in contact with the corner of a cabin. I shouted "Hello!" but heard no answer. I continued feeling until I came to the door and found that a board was nailed across it. The cabin was locked and deserted! I broke in the door.

In the cabin I found a stove and wood. As soon as I had a fire going I dropped snow upon the stove and steamed my painful eyes. After two hours or more of this steaming they became more comfortable. Two strenuous days and one toilsome night had made me extremely drowsy. Sitting down upon the floor near the stove I leaned against the wall and fell asleep. But the fire burned itself out. In the night I awoke nearly frozen and unable to rise. Fortunately, I had on my mittens, otherwise my fingers probably would have frozen. By rubbing my hands together, then rubbing my arms and legs, I finally managed to limber myself, and though unable to rise, I succeeded in starting a new fire. It was more than an hour before I ceased shivering; then, as the room began to warm, my legs came back to life and again I could walk.

I was hungry. This was my first thought of food since becoming blind. If there was anything to eat in the cabin, I failed to find it. Searching my pockets I found a dozen or more raisins and with these I broke my sixty hour fast. Then I had another sleep, and it must have been near noon when I awakened. Again I steamed the eye pain into partial submission.

Going to the door I stood and listened. A camp-bird only a few feet away spoke gently and confidingly. Then a crested jay called impatiently. The camp-bird alighted on my shoulder. I tried to explain to the birds that there was nothing to eat. The prospector who had lived in this cabin evidently had been friendly with the bird neighbors. I wished that I might know him.

Again I could smell the smoke of aspen wood. Several shouts evoked echoes—nothing more. I stood listening and wondering whether to stay in the cabin or to venture forth and try to follow the snow-filled roadway that must lead down through the woods from the cabin. Wherever this open way led I could follow, but of course I must take care not to lose it.

In the nature of things I felt that I must be three or four miles to the south of the trail which I had planned to follow down the mountain. I wished I might see my long and crooked line of footmarks in the snow from the summit to timberline.

Hearing the open water in rapids close to the cabin, I went out to try for a drink. I advanced slowly, blind-man fashion, feeling the way with my long staff. As I neared the rapids, a water ouzel, which probably had lunched in the open water, sang with all his might. I stood still as he repeated his liquid, hopeful song. On the spot I shook off procrastination and decided to try to find a place where someone lived.

After writing a note explaining why I had smashed in the door and used so much wood, I readjusted my snowshoes and started down through the woods. I suppose it must have been late afternoon.

I found an open way that had been made into a road. The woods were thick and the open roadway readily guided me. Feeling and thrusting with my staff, I walked for some time at normal pace. Then I missed the way. I searched carefully, right, left, and before me for the utterly lost road. It had forked, and I had continued on the short stretch that came to an end in the woods by an abandoned prospect hole. As I approached close to this the snow caved in, nearly carrying me along with it. Confused by blinded eyes and the thought of oncoming night, perhaps, I had not used my wits. When at last I stopped to think, I figured out the situation. Then I followed my snowshoe tracks back to the main road and turned into it.

For a short distance the road ran through dense woods. Several times I paused to touch the trees each side with my hands. When I emerged from the woods, the pungent aspen smoke said that I must at last be near a human habitation. In fear of passing it I stopped to use my ears. As I stood listening, a little girl gently, curiously, asked:

"Are you going to stay here tonight?"

Travelers above timberline, Rocky Mountain National Park.

Waiting in the wilderness, that is, lingering in a spot frequently visited by wild life, appears to be one of the easiest and most delightful ways of getting acquainted with nature and the ways of the wild.

Going repeatedly to the same place means the visiting of an old scene in which changes are constantly taking place during your absence and in which the beginning of something new may occur while you are there. So, to have a really intimate and happy acquaintance and a most thorough appreciation of the wild world stage, one must revisit the same stage again and again.

—Enos A. Mills

Waiting in the Wilderness

They were a pair of hairy woodpeckers engaged in examining a fourteen-inch dead aspen. As it was nesting time I lingered to watch them. After taking a number of grubs from beneath the bark of the tree the birds centered their woodpecking work at one spot, about a man's height above the roots.

Mrs. Woodpecker pecked a number of tiny holes or dots, forming a circle about two inches in diameter. Then she pecked and hammered away within this circle. Presently this space began to take on the form of a doorway or entrance hole to a nest. Chips and broken bits flew. The birds worked rapidly, one at a time. While Mrs. Woodpecker worked, her mate watched nearby and tried two or three times to take a hand, but she thrust him aside and kept on pecking and hammering until at last she grew tired and his turn came. After three hours a sizeable impression was made in the tree and both birds flew away into the aspen grove. I waited half an hour, but they did not come back. After spending more than an hour looking over a beaver house on the bank of a brook, distant a stone's throw, I returned to the aspen, but the woodpeckers were still away.

The aspen grove in which these birds were working stood within the seclusion of a mountain forest. Nearby ran a brook from west to east. To the south of the brook, behind the aspen grove, a spruce forest covered the slope. On the north a pine woods stretched away. Between the pine wood and the brook was a grassy opening with a pile of boulders. Through the grove and across the brook ran a wildlife trail.

Busy was the life in the woods. I had frequent glimpses of wildlife folk, an occasional view of a one act play in which any number of performers took lively part. Close to me at one time a weasel, aggressive as a lion, killed a number of mice, and at another time I saw a weasel kill a chipmunk. Among the birds and small animals there were comedies, courtships, feasts, fights, and frolics. All took place in a bit of the wild across which a primitive man could have hurled his spear.

The unexpected often happened. The hours never dragged, they were enlivened by a succession of incidents and episodes. Again and again I enjoyed this primeval, poetic place for hours, while I sat unmoved and watchful in the scene. Often I lay on a log or on the ground, or hid in the bushes, or sometimes simply stood like a stump. Wherever I might be, without moving I let ants crawl over me and insects bite me as they would. Frequently there was a shower of rain, which when not accompanied by wind or lightning had a softening, subduing effect upon all the forest sounds.

Two days after I had first observed the woodpecker home-makers, I found them working industriously in the hole which was now more than three inches deep. Only a part of the chips flew out of the hole as they were cut, the rest were swept out from time to time by Mr. Woodpecker. This feat he performed by leaning back and turning his head quickly, his bill acting as the broom.

Woodpeckers often select the aspen for a nesting site, probably because of its soft, easily worked wood. Frequently they take dead, partly decayed trees, in which nests are most easily made; and dead trees, too, often are filled with grubs, ants, and other woodpecker food.

By the fifth day the woodpeckers had cut the hole to a depth of about seven inches. The workers continued at their task and finished the nest to average size. After excavating seven inches into the tree the entrance way curved downward into the trunk to a depth of about twelve inches, the lower section having a diameter of six inches. All this was the work of eleven days.

The woodpecker's nest is one of the cleanest and safest and

probably the most continuously comfortable of all birds' nests. It keeps out the rain and excludes the extremes of cold and heat. It is perhaps less likely to be discovered by enemies than the nest of any other bird. Rarely does an accident befall it. What a strange, cunning place for young birds to grow up in! How interested they must be the first time they climb up and from the doorway peep into the strange wilderness world.

Nearly a month elapsed before I was again in the aspen grove. When I tapped lightly on the woodpecker's tree four agitated bills were thrust out of the doorway. But as they saw nothing to eat the four red-topped youngsters withdrew their bills and, I suppose, settled back to the bottom of the nest. Presently one of the old birds appeared, and instantly bills receivable were again presented through the doorway. After feeding one of the youngsters the old bird eyed me for a moment with a peculiar look—suggesting curiosity, however, rather than fear. It flew away and a moment later its mate arrived with a grub in its bill.

I missed the pleasure of seeing the young woodpeckers leave the nest and make their baby start in the wooded world. One October day I was back in the grove and paused to watch, as usual, the continuous though ever-changing performances. While I was

A spot in an aspen grove filled with wildflowers.

standing near the nest tree a busy chipmunk climbed up and peeped into the deserted woodpecker nest. Then he climbed up a few feet higher, went round the tree and came back to the nest. After several times thrusting in his head and forefeet—each time withdrawing quickly and retreating almost to the grass—he finally found courage and bravely entered. Out rushed a frightened field mouse. A few moments later the chipmunk thrust out his head and with feet on the edge of the entrance hole he looked round like a young lion. The nest became his winter quarters. One day a month later I saw him again thrust his head from this adopted nest. Tracks in the snow at the foot of the tree showed that he came out occasionally.

The following May when I called, a pair of bluebirds were striking and beating at the chipmunk, who was clinging to the tree trunk near the nest entrance. The chipmunk finally leaped off and retreated into the grove, with the birds in pursuit. Again and again I came to linger at my old place. During the summer five baby bluebirds were raised in this nest. After they were safely brought off and taken in charge by Mr. Bluebird, the mother bird again filled the nest with eggs.

I did not make my rounds again until summer was over. When I returned, the chipmunk who occupied it the previous year, or a chipmunk of the same species and about the same size, was in the nest. More likely it was the same chipmunk, for when I threw a peanut to him he made haste to pick it up—a trick he had learned during my visits the year previous.

The next spring in the grove I heard a wren singing with all his might. What busy, happy, aggressive, and confiding little folk wrens are! I was glad when I found that Mr. and Mrs. Wren would keep house for the summer in the woodpecker nest. A robin was a near neighbor, nesting on the top of a high, broken pine stump. Often while I lay or stood watching the wrens, a camp-bird—the Rocky Mountain gray jay—came to see me, plainly with the hope that I would have a bite of something to offer. Of all the birds that I have seen, none on first sight is so trustful of man as is the camp-bird.

That winter and the following summer I often saw a tiny owl

come out of the woodpecker's old nest, where a pair of owls must have been nesting, I think. Anyway, for more than a year it was their wooden-walled home.

That year a pair of woodpeckers had a nest in the upper end of the aspen grove. As they allowed me to approach more closely than other hairy woodpeckers, I believe they were my former acquaintances whom I had watched two years before.

In the upper end of the grove another pair of hairy woodpeckers had a nest, nearly twenty feet above the ground, which they had evidently used for three summers in succession. A short distance down the brook I one day came upon an abandoned woodpecker nest—probably that of a sapsucker. It was not more than three feet above the ground. Two summers later it was occupied by a pair of hairy woodpeckers.

One day, hearing a rather alarmed "peek, peek," and thinking that something was happening to one of the woodpeckers, I made haste to the brook, where I saw two kingfishers looking upstream. The alarm cry of these birds is very like that of the hairy woodpecker. There on a log sat a mink, evidently the cause of the excitement. The view I had of these kingfishers' heads as they stood up reminded me of the heads of two football players. Returning from this inspection I was astonished to see a flicker alight on the nest tree and take a peek into the doorway of the woodpecker nest. The arrival of one of the bird owners made him take a hurried leave.

There are three hundred and fifty known species of woodpeckers in the world. They are found nearly everywhere that there are trees and in a few treeless places. I believe that there are no woodpeckers in Australia. Of the twenty-five species found in North America one of the smaller and more common is the hairy woodpecker. He is a valuable bird and saves many a tree from insect death.

The Rocky Mountain hairy woodpecker has a length of about nine inches. Although he is whitish beneath, with grayish legs, the general effect when he is at rest is blackish. The outer tail feathers are white-tipped and the wings show spots of white. Just above and below the eye is a narrow white stripe, and a narrow white and

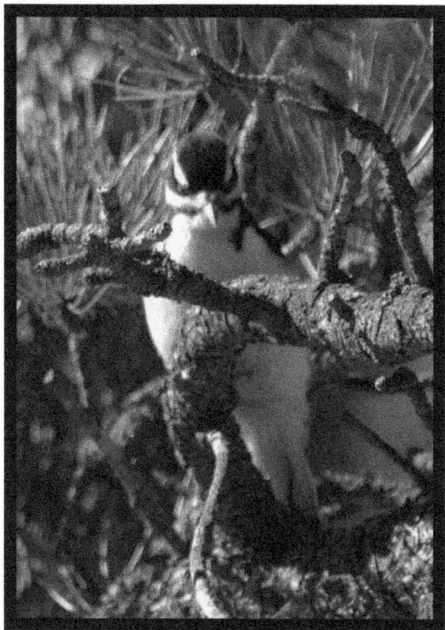

This page:
A female hairy
woodpecker.
Photos by
Eryn V. Mills

red stripe crosses the back of the head. The youngsters commonly have a reddish top.

The food of the hairy woodpecker consists of wood borers, spiders, moths, ants, and occasionally berries. Though they summer and nest in high altitudes—often nearly eleven thousand feet above sea level—they commonly descend the mountains with the approach of winter and spend the cooler months among the foothills. The Rocky Mountain hairy woodpecker is not so fond of living in orchards and being near people as is his cousin the downy. Although human visitors to his home region do not annoy him he plainly enjoys the seclusion of pathless forests.

These woodpeckers probably mate for life, and are quietly devoted, enjoying each other's company without demonstration. For a week or two in late spring Mr. Hairy Woodpecker is noisy enough. He simply fills the woods with drumming, drumming.

He calls and calls merrily, with many a change of tone. Often it is keak-keak-keak-kick-kick, whit-whit-whit-whi-wi-wi-i-i-wi. But as soon as the white eggs are laid—there are from three to six in number—he does his full share of incubating them.

I was standing in an open space one day, watching the movements of a squirrel, when I chanced to see coming toward me Mrs. Skunk and three pretty little skunkies. As these skunks came closer it looked as though I might move shortly. They were walking leisurely, apparently going to a definite place, and all carried their tails elevated at a decorative social angle. Naturally I did not wish to dispute their right to the trail. I held my ground from sheer willpower. They concluded to take a little passageway about six feet in front of me. I stood like a statue to watch them go by. In passing Mrs. Skunk tilted her head and looked at me out of one eye, but without changing her pace or saying anything to the children, kept on her way. Nothing happened, but never before did I borrow so much trouble in a few seconds. About thirty feet beyond me Mother Skunk paused and dug out a mouse.

Squirrels were about. A Fremont squirrel lived in the pines to the south of my watching place, another a short distance to the north. This little gray fellow is closely related to the Douglas squirrel of California. He is one of the smallest of the squirrel family. He is fiery, curious, and wide-awake. He has as much courage and individuality to his inches as any animal I have ever seen. I often heard one of these squirrels as he clucked, chattered, or talked to himself. Occasionally he denounced with terrific violence a passing animal or intruder.

The first few days that I watched proceedings in the grove the squirrel nearest to my station showed immense curiosity. He was unable to make out what I was about. One day he rushed at me and with a savage outburst threatened either to devour me or to kick me off his premises. As I remained silent and motionless he paused in astonishment. Then he backed up and eyed me eagerly. Again he tried bluff and denunciation. At last, doubtless wondering why I was not moving and whether I should remain long, he gave it up, climbed into his tree, and proceeded with his own affairs.

One day when swarm of bees started to light upon me I made a lively retreat. This disturbed Mr. Squirrel. He broke out in volleys of peppery chatter that lasted for two or three minutes, then he subsided and sat looking at me. I imagined that he might be thinking or saying to himself, "Well, for the life of me, this is something I cannot understand!"

From dawn until dusk I once watched the activities of this fellow. Though he was sometimes temporarily out of sight I waited, wondering what the next move would be.

He climbed into the treetops and cut off cones which fell, bounced, and rolled away, and appeared to try to land where he could not find them. Often he stopped to look and listen and make sure that no outsider was capturing his cones.

My squirrel friend had a sad end. Lightning one day struck a tree frequented by him, on the south side of the stream, and killed him. The bolt literally knocked the head off this tree and it threw half a dozen young birds out of a nest in a tree nearby. Evidently this other tree had been struck twice before. A few years previously a bolt had run down one side, bursting the bark. Through this break a number of beetles had made their way to begin work on the vitals of the tree. Chief Surgeon Woodpecker was often there, and in a length of sixteen feet along this broken trunk had made sixteen holes and had probably removed many a borer.

Once I saw a large, dignified mountain sheep walk quietly across the grassy opening. He did not see me. On reaching the farther edge he turned about, recrossed the opening to the boulder pile and leaped upon it. After remaining there, statuesque, awhile, he reentered the woods, stood for a moment, and then disappeared.

It was impossible to feel lonesome. Eyes and ears were kept busy for the show went ever on. It was a one-ring, a three-ring, sometimes a six-ring show all at once. Too often a number of extra good things were going on together. A squirrel would be up to something, while at the same instant two chipmunks would be having a boundary line dispute. Along with these a robin might be noisy and pessimistic over something that may not have happened, while a rare warbler that I wanted to see was darting about in the treetops, and a porcupine was waddling by with dull deliberation.

The birds on the other side of the brook one afternoon set up a great ado, as if some enemy were about to raid them or some other terror were nigh. Of them all, the most excited and pessimistic was the mother robin. She flew and darted about without getting anywhere, all the time predicting the worst possible calamity. When things had almost calmed down a broad-tailed hummingbird came flying by, scolding hard, plainly much put out because of all this unnecessary hullabaloo. After darting about me for some seconds, with her burnished body flashing and bead-like eyes shining, she alighted like any bird on a neighboring limb. This midget made a comical appearance, aping, as it seemed, all the poses of a real sized bird.

Once I looked round just in time to see a coyote leap forward and land upon the grass with forepaws together. Presently he thrust in his nose and pulled out a mouse. At this instant he caught sight of me and edged off sideways, eying me intently. He was not frightened, but apparently could not make out what I was or what I was doing. He passed, doubled, and repassed nearby. Then he circled, and when he caught my scent, sniffed the air but still was not alarmed. He stayed to watch, like a boy in no hurry who had found something new. In the edge of the opening he stretched out on his stomach with his head toward me. Occasionally his nostrils

21

twitched a little, but at no time did he look upon me with fear or suspicion. Soon sounded a whack from the nearby beaver pond, as if a beaver had dived, and a second later came muffled footfalls through the forest from the opposite quarter. These alarms caused Mr. Coyote to leap up all alert, and presently he hastened away among the shadows.

A number of deer came to visit the place. After eying me closely from a distance of thirty or forty feet they lingered to look round and to take an occasional bite to eat. They were curious about me, but were perfectly at ease, for they had not scented me. Another day three deer, which had not seen me, suddenly caught scent of me and were off instantly. Most animals rely upon their noses for chief scout duty to tell them when to flee for safety. Deer, beavers, and sometimes other animals which saw me without scenting me, simply took a brief look, then continued their affairs in a normal manner; but usually when they scented me before seeing me they were alarmed and thought that "safety first" required speed.

A mother grouse and her family of youngsters came along while I was sitting on a log. I kept perfectly still. One of the youngsters jumped up on the log and started toward me. Two or three walked close to me, and some of the others passed between my legs and the log. Evidently they took me for a bump or a stump. The mother bird was behind, walking vigilantly and with stately dignity. The youngster on the log came up to me and pecked at a button on my coat. I turned to look. This told the mother that I was alive. It suggested danger. She instantly flung herself at me and struck me a slap on the side of the head. Dropping back she again lunged and beat me with her wings. Her brave behaviour was very like that of a hen in the defense of her chicks.

Once, just before sundown, a solitaire lighted on a tall spruce top and poured forth his elemental and eloquent song. It was divinely beautiful in the evening hush of the wilderness. He sang with all his melody and all his might. Often in his enthusiasm he hurled himself upward or outward from the treetop, then settled or returned on easy, outstretched wings, singing all the time. No song that I have ever heard so harmonizes with the silences and the feeling of a mountain wilderness or so completely puts one in tune with the universe as the marvelous melody of the solitaire.

Momentarily one day I took my eyes from the woodpeckers. A rabbit came hopping along, completely unmindful of my presence, passed me, and presently disappeared among the trees. A minute later a soft-footed coyote came following on the rabbit's trail. Though so near he evidently did not see me, but hurried along and disappeared behind an old pine. I do not know what happened.

On another occasion a flutter of wings and a chirp caused me to turn. Near me a little chickadee was working away at a hole in a dead snag and was just in the act of spitting out a mouthful of dead wood. Here was another nest builder.

Once a black bear came along and stopped under the pines on a knoll not far from me. Here he rolled over an old ant-filled log. Out rushed ferociously about a million ants, which the bear licked up rapidly, with a pleased expression. Presently he came a little closer to me and dug out a mouse. Then he flushed a number of grasshoppers; but in leaping into the air and striking at one of these on the wing he scented me and at once beat a retreat.

One day I left my old watching place and climbed the heights. As usual I moved quietly and slowly, and once on the skyline I paused to look around. Lying near a spring in the center of the terrace was a deer. As I watched her, nibbling at the plants around her, from the position of one of her legs I judged that it was broken, probably by a bullet. Suddenly the wind warned her that a deadly enemy was near. Instantly she leaped up, forgetful of her broken bones. She stood and smelled, but without discovering me. Watching my chance I slipped away. I had not gone far before darkness advised stopping and I spent the night by a fire without bedding.

Next morning, advancing in the breeze, I climbed up to watch the doe. She lay still nearly all day. Most of the time her ears moved nervously about as she caught sounds from this way and that. When an eagle soared overhead she showed much uneasiness but moved only eyes and ears. In midafternoon she was startled by the fall of a rock mass down one of the crags nearby. A short time after this some mountain sheep appeared on the skyline above, posed, and looked quietly around. From the actions of the sheep the doe evidently concluded that all was well. She struggled slowly to her feet, giving a low call as she rose. Soon I knew that a fawn was having a warm meal. I do not know where the fawn had been hidden. Realizing that the deer should not be disturbed for some days I moved on to enjoy other scenes and left her in possession.

Among the actors who appeared where I next watched were a bear and her two boyish cubs. A peppery, curious Fremont squirrel in a tree nearby saw them approach. He ceased work, eyed them for a time with lively curiosity then with apparent contempt. At last he went on with his work without voicing a protest until later, when the cubs engaged in a playful scuffle.

Mother bear lumbered along under the trees, unaware or indifferent that the squirrel, apparently in his own estimation one of the most ferocious animals in the wilds, might leap down upon her. At one place she stopped, thrust a forepaw beneath the up-turned roots of a fallen tree, and, with a lift and a push, thrust the heavy, bulky mass aside. She licked the earth a few times, probably to pick up some bugs or ants, and then started on.

The cubs dropped behind and began digging; they were having a beautiful time. The mother paused, looked, and went back to see what it was all about. They were working with great zest, and she apparently supposed that they had scented something worth while. In the rudest manner she pushed each aside, smelled in the hole, found nothing, and at once started on. The cubs followed.

They came so close to me that I thought surely they would either see me or scent me, but they passed me by unnoticed and a short distance away found chokecherry bushes on the side of a ravine. The mother bear at once began feasting on the puckery ripe berries. Evidently she cared nothing for conservation, for she crushed down and bit off the bushes. She rose on her hind feet and with mouth and claws together grasped at the laden ends of the branches. Limb ends, leaves, berries—all were devoured.

Chokecherries evidently were a desert for which her young-sters did not care. The berries may have been new to them. At any rate, two bites satisfied them. The bulging, rounded little stomachs plainly indicated many helpings of other eatables. Even a bear cub can be filled up.

For a time they lay relaxed in the sun. Then they rose, stood up, and showed off. They struck out like green, awkward boxers. They struck at nothing or sometimes with both paws held low and at an angle, and sometimes with one paw held high. Then they had a wrestling match—clinching, hugging, and rolling. Their first belligerent attitude brought rather a vehement protest from the squirrel, who quickly subsided, however, and became a silent spectator. A camp-bird also looked on, watching them from the limb of a pine. He observed closely, but did not appear enthusiastic over the exhibition.

What a number of incidents in this little area! Quite as many may also happen in countless other small spaces. Often I wondered about things that took place when I was away; what quiet, interesting, unseen incidents that I never even suspected were ever occurring.

The aspen grove round the woodpeckers' nest was made up of trees from six to fifteen inches in diameter and thirty to sixty feet high. Most of their bark was milk-white. Under the trees were a few bushes and many grassy spaces in which violets, columbines, harebells, gentians, and other flowers bloomed.

In summer butterflies with painted wings floated and circled over the sunny opening. Rarely did they fold their wings and alight. Occasionally one sailed through the woods, following a fairy avenue. Its bright, beautiful color gave a charm and an illumination to the forest gloom. Bees visited the flowers, and occasionally a bumblebee buzzed hurriedly through, as if in desperate haste to reach a certain place and knowing well his destination. Grasshoppers, too, in the autumn days enlivened the scene. Occasionally a huge fellow leaped out of the grass with a crackling and the flash of color like a fairy rocket before he settled back.

Often I was in the grove when the snowflakes fell; and I saw the colored leaves fall one by one. Grandly the moon shone in these scenes. Early morning and evening lights under the trees and through the woods were strange and beautiful. They put the trees at their best and in attitudes different from those shown in the down-pouring light of midday.

The aspen grove where I frequently watched the manners and customs of our wild kindred was a much better place in which to study natural history than that afforded by any zoo. I wish that a company of boys and girls might have been with me. How they would have enjoyed these real nature stories! I am sure they would have been happy. But, thanks to the Audubon Society, to other organizations, and to numerous individuals, boys and girls are beginning to watch, enjoy, and receive the benefits of knowing the wild people of the wood who dress in fur and feathers.

Yes, Mother Nature conducts a delightful outdoor school and it is open every day in the year. Wherever there is a bit of wildness there are pretty certain to be numerous interesting little wild people. Of course bird reservations are even better places for this kind of schooling and fun. The greatest of all places for these advantages are our national parks.

Surely one of the best pastimes for children—for anyone—is to wait at a wildlife center and watch the ways of its residents and its visitors. To do this is pleasant self-discipline. It is constructive. It keeps the eyes open and the senses alert. It gives material for thought and compels thinking. It arouses the imagination and wakes up the creative faculties. The faculty of keen observation, the ability to see accurately, and the incentive to watch for things that may happen around us, add much to every outdoor day. Such happy experiences as these truly enrich life.

"In his later American travels he would talk of glacial phenomena to the driver of a country stagecoach among the mountains, or to some workman, splitting rock at the road-side, with as much earnestness as if he had been discussing problems with a brother geologist; he would take the common fisherman into his scientific confidence, telling him the intimate secrets of fish-structure or fish-embryology, till the man in his turn became enthusiastic, and began to pour out information from the stores of his own rough and untaught habits of observation. Agassiz's general faith in the susceptibility of the popular intelligence, however untrained, to the highest truths of nature, was contagious, and he created or developed that in which he believed."

—Elizabeth Cary Agassiz

Winter Mountaineering

After a heavy snowfall one December morning, I started on skis for two weeks' camping in the Colorado Rockies. The fluffy snow lay smooth and unbroken over the broken mountains. Here and there black pine and spruce trees uplifted arrowheads and snow cones of the white mantle. On the steep slope, half a mile from my cabin, I was knocked to one side by a barrel mass of snow dropping upon me from a tree, and one ski escaped. As if glad to be off on an adventure of its own, it sped down the mountainside like a shot. It bumped into a low stump, skied high into the air and over a treetop, and then fell undamaged in the deep snow.

Recovering my runaway ski, I started for the summit of the range, a distance of about nine miles from my cabin. For an hour I followed a stream whose swift waters now and then splashed up through the broken, icy skylights. Then leaving the canyon and skirting the slope, I was on the plateau summit of the Continental Divide, twelve thousand feet above the sea.

This summit moor was deeply overlaid with undrifted snow. Southward it extended mile after mile, rising higher and higher into the sky in broken, snow-covered peaks. To the north the few small broken cliffs and low buttes emphasized the trackless solitude. This plateau or moorland was less than one mile wide and comparatively smooth. Its edges descended precipitously two thousand feet into cirques and canyons.

Southward I traveled along the nearly level expanse of undrifted snow. Looking back along the line of my ski tracks, I saw a mountain lion leisurely cross from east to west. Apparently she had come up out of the woods for mad play and slaughter among the unfortunate snow-bound folk of the summit. She stopped at my tracks for an interested look, turned her head, and glanced back along the way I had come. Then her eyes appeared to follow my tracks to the boulder pile from behind which I was then looking.

Playfully bouncing off the snow, she struck into my ski prints with one forepaw, lightly as a kitten. Then she dived into them, pretended to pick up something between her forepaws, reared, and with a swing tossed it into the air. Then her playful mood changed and she started on across the Divide. After several steps she stopped, looking back as if she had forgotten something but was a little too lazy to retrace her steps. But finally she came back. She walked along my ski tracks for a few steps, then began to romp, now and then making a great leap forward, and rolled and struck about with the pretense of worrying something she had captured. She repeated this pantomime a few times, and then, as if suddenly remembering her original plan of action, again walked westward. Arriving at the summit she hesitated, and when I saw her last she was calmly surveying the scenes far below.

On the mountain skyline I crossed a white tundra, half expecting to see an Eskimo peer from a snow mound. Arctic plants buried in the snow and ptarmigan—"Eskimo chickens"—in their snow-white dress were the only signs of life. Later in the day I saw a white weasel slipping over the snow toward a number of the ptarmigan. Often on the summits the ptarmigan, in leggings and coats of pure white, watched me and allowed me to come and remain near. They, like the snowshoe rabbit, skimmed over the surface on home-grown snowshoes. Possibly from them the Eskimos got the idea for the webbed snowshoe, which they have used for ages. More than once, when weathering gales were thick, insistent snow dust made me acquainted with the unpleasant sensations of strangulation, I have envied the rosy finch and other birds of the snow who have a well-developed screen to keep choking snow dust out of the nostrils. The Eskimos also have a slotted wooden shield to protect the eye from the burning glare of reflected sunlight.

I descended a few hundred feet into the upper edge of the woods to find shelter for the night. Clearing out the snow between a cliff and a rock about six feet from it, I had an excellent lodging place. I built a roaring fire and heated a number of stones. When this space was warmed I pushed the fire and the heated stones along the open space between the rock and the cliff. Then I started a fire against the base of the detached rock. Two huge sticks were placed at the bottom of this fire pile. Over these smaller ones were laid, and at the top still smaller ones. I set fire to this on the top so that it would burn slowly and not be at its hottest for an hour or two. Within the circle of warmth I placed my elkskin sleeping bag, crawled into it, and slept for nearly four hours. When the cold awakened me I renewed both fires, then had another short sleep. When I again awoke I was ready for another day's adventure.

I set off through a forested slope that tilted gently toward the sun. Black shadows, long and straight, lay upon the forest floor. The crowded pines were slender and limbless except at the top. Across an opening these slender shadows were at their best, with the snow glistening in white lines between their deep black ones. After two hours I came out upon a white and treeless meadow, across which shadows were flying—moving cloud shadows rushed across, and the shadow of a soaring eagle appeared swiftly skating in circles over the snow.

I spent hours reading the news, observing the illustrations, and studying the hieroglyphics on the snow. Whether footprints in the mud or snow may have suggested printing cannot be told, but it is certain that the tracks, stains and impressions in snow print the news and record the local animal doings. Here the rabbits played; there the grouse searched for dinner; while over yonder the long, lacy trail of a mouse ends significantly between the impressions of two wing feathers. One sees a trail made by a long-legged animal and another by a fellow with a long body and short legs—perhaps a weasel. At one place near the foot of an old tree a squirrel had abandoned a cone and run home. Nearby was the trail of a porcupine who was well-fed, well-protected, and though dull-witted, not at all afraid. Apparently he hadn't any idea where he was going and did not care whom he should meet; for at one place he came face to face with a fox and the fox turned aside.

Footprints often reveal the excitement, hesitation, change of plan, and the preparation of two wild folks advancing and about to meet. Most animals, except the grizzly, though concerned with sight and scent, appear not to consider the impressions in the tell-tale snow.

I passed again through woods where the previous winter I had walked upon ten feet of snow. In that trip I had looked down upon a camp-bird cuddled in an old nest. I talked to her for a minute, and, as is common with her kind, she came close, seeking something to eat. Three eggs were in the nest, though it was February. Never before had I found a bird nesting in the famine month of the year. These eggs may not have hatched, but another time I saw a nest of this species in March with eggs that did hatch. April is the nesting time for this bird. Why a pair sometimes nest unusually early is their secret.

I found the crested jay, that flings forth its jarring note as harsh and cold as frosty steel, using these mountains for winter quarters. A few of this species remain for the summer, but the majority nest farther north. The water ouzel is a winter songster, and twice during this outing, in a snow-filled canyon, he sang to me cheerily. He may be seen and heard in any month of the year. This bird of quiet, cheering presence is an outdoor enthusiast. He was always delightfully busy, and indifferent to my close approach if I came quietly and slowly.

The scarlet berries and small, shining green leaves of the kinnikinick gave color and charm to many snowy places. Half buried in the snow, in the sun or shadow, in niches of crags, or as wreath-like coverings for the rocks, they were bright and cheerful everywhere.

I can imagine that the winter birds and animals worship the chinook wind. One evening I went to sleep shivering. I was awakened through being too warm, and leaped out of my sleeping bag thinking it must be on fire. Then I discovered that in the night a chinook had come. This warm, dry wind occasionally follows a blizzard, and often it appears to make a sudden and triumphant attack upon a cold period. During the short day or two that it dominates it is a blessing. It often raises the temperature thirty or more degrees in a few hours.

On another cold, windy night I had a poor camp and damp clothes. I had examined the ice around a beaver house to see if it was built by a spring. It was, and I had broken through the thin ice. That night as I shivered by a slow fire I wished that I might have occupied a woodpecker's house. I took comfort in the fact that at no time during the trip would I be annoyed by flies or mosquitoes.

From the sheltering edge of the woods I watched the high wind stir and sweep the excited snow. The snowflakes had long since been reduced to powder and dust by colliding with cliffs and by being thrown violently against the earth. The wind was intermittent. A wave of snow dust swept along the snow-crusted earth, filling the air; then a few seconds of sunshine played before the next wave followed. Occasionally everything cleared and stopped for an exhibit of the whirlwind. A towering white column of snow dust would spin across the scene. This commonly was followed by another and heavier spiral that was more like a confusion of white whirled clouds. All this time the sun was shining in a blue sky; and all this time, too, a sparkling pennant of diamond snow dust and powder a mile long was fluttering from the tip of a triangular peak.

With such scenes in mind—the trees abloom with flakes, the white and sparkling whirlwinds, the vast and scintillating snow-powder pennants—I could understand the poetic fancy of primitive people who happily named the winter's gifts "snow-flowers" and who honored the snow period with an outdoor celebration.

After all, winter is but a transient return of the ice age. With fresh falls on the heights above timberline, before the wind blows, the vast world appears overlaid with a permanent stratum of snow. Across white distances one looks for miles without seeing a tree or any living object or even a shadow unless it be that of a passing cloud.

Though the high mountains have their snowstorms and their eternal snowfields, in most mountain ranges the snowfall on the middle slopes of the mountains is heavier than upon the high plateaus and summits. On the heights the wind has free play and sweeps most of the snow into enormous piles or drifts. These are one hundred or more feet deep and sometimes cover nearly a square mile. Owing to their depth, the low temperature of the heights, and the fact that they are so densely packed, these snow masses endure throughout the year. Wind is thus the chief factor in the making of snow topography. Small hills and plains, canyons, plateaus, and mountain ranges—all of snow—are a constant source of interest.

One morning I awoke with dense, white storm clouds all around me and the snow coming down. Wishing to camp that night at timberline, I traveled up the mountainside in the thickly falling snow and dense clouds. These clouds were drifting easily along the mountainside and, together with the feathery flakes which they were shedding, made it impossible to see distinctly even to the end of an extended arm. Suddenly I became aware of a diminished depth of snow underfoot. I stooped to measure it. It was less than three inches. On rising I thrust my head through the silver lining—the upper surface—of the cloud into the sunshine.

The altitude was about eleven thousand feet. Above and about me the peaks and plateaus stood in gray and brown. Not a flake of all this snow had fallen upon them. There was nothing to indicate that a storm had prevailed just below during the last two days and nights, or that only a step down the mountain snow was still falling.

Soundless and motionless the cloud sea lay below. Here and there an upthrusting pinnacle cast a shadow upon it. Unable to make myself believe that below me the flakes were falling thick and fast and that the ground was deeply covered with soft white snow, I plunged down into the cloud. After enjoying the novelty for a few minutes I climbed out of the snowstorm again and then once more descended into it. As the mountainside was comparatively unbroken I walked along the upper edge of the cloud for some distance. Two or three times this fluffy mass swelled and rose slightly above me and then settled easily back. In the head of a gulch cloud swells rose slightly higher than out in the main sea. I climbed down into them a short distance, thinking to cross the hidden canyon, but, finding it too steep-walled, climbed out again.

As I emerged from the gulch I saw, nearby, a huge grizzly bear sunning himself on a cliff that rose a few feet out of the cloud into the sunshine. He, like myself, appeared greatly interested in the slow rise and fall and ragged outline of the storm cloud. He was all attention to every new movement near him. On scenting me he stared for a moment, as if thinking: "Where on earth did he come from?" Then he stepped overboard into the clouds.

I camped that night beside a clump of storm-battered trees that marked the upper limit of the forest. In the morning all was clear. The cloud sea of the day before had rolled silently away. Along the mountainside the ragged edge of snow stretched for miles. Above it barren, rocky peaks rose in a great mountain desert. Below, all was soft and white—a wonderful world of mountains made of snowflakes.

Near my camp was an ancient looking tree clump. None of the trees was taller than my head, and though of almost normal form they were somewhat gnarled and appeared as old as the hills. Centuries they surely had seen. Trees on the forest outpost in high mountains endure severe trials. They are dwarfed, battered, and broken; huddled behind boulders, buried, or half buried in snow. The forest frontier is maintained by these brave tree people. Seen again and again, this region displays features of new interest as often as the visitor returns to it.

On the heights I frequently saw conies. One day I lingered to watch one that was less shy than the majority. He sat with his back against the sunny side of a boulder, looking serious and keeping a careful survey of his field of vision. Presently I discovered his haystack—his supply of winter food—a tiny heap of grass, sedge, and alpine plants. It was about two feet high and was sheltered beneath two half-arching stones.

Many were the ways in which I found animals spending the winter. In the course of this outing I saw several flocks of mountain sheep. All these were in the heights above the tree line. On the day following the snow-drifting one I crossed the heights and on the summit passed close to a flock. They were feeding in a space that the wind had swept bare of snow. Happy highlanders they were, well fed and contented, in their home twelve thousand feet above the tides.

One sunny, though cold, morning I came upon a large, dead tree. In it were a number of woodpecker holes. Wondering if these houses had winter dwellers I struck the tree with my hatchet. Instantly a dozen or more chickadees came pouring out of one of the holes like so many merry children. From a hole in the opposite side to the tree flew one or more birds that I did not see. Out of one of the upper holes a downy woodpecker thrust his head. Glaring down at me with one eye—impatient, as late sleepers usually are when called—he appeared to be wanting to say: "Why am I disturbed? This is a cold morning. There are no early worms to be had in winter." From another hole flew another downy. I felt sure that none of these late sleepers had breakfasted. Seldom is an old woodpecker house without a tenant. Bluebirds, wrens, and numbers of weak-billed folk nest in them during summer, while birds of other species find them life-savers in the winter. A hummingbird's nest that I found brought to mind the fact that its builder, if alive, was then among the tropical flowers of Central America.

Later in the day I saw a flock of chickadees, one or two brown creepers, and a solitary woodpecker food hunting together. The chickadees kept up a cheering conversation and twice I thought I heard the woodpecker give a call. I wondered if these fellow food hunters also all lodged in one many-roomed apartment house.

Coming one day to a beaver pond I scraped off the snow and looked through the clear ice into the water. Two or three beavers were swimming. The water between the ice and the bottom of the pond was about two feet deep. Each autumn the beavers pile ample winter supplies in deep water close to the house. The pond may freeze over, but this ice covering is a protection. The house entrance is on the bottom of the pond beneath the ice, and the floor is above the level of the pond. The water in the lower part of the house does not freeze. The beaver residents were here having a comfortable time while deer in nearby woods were floundering in the snow. I have known deer to have a hard time of it in winter. Commonly deer winter in lower altitudes, but sometimes they stay in the middle mountain region and worry through the snowy weeks by yarding—that is, a number remaining in one small area, where through daily trampling they keep on top of the snow and still find enough to eat.

A number of animals hibernate. Fat woodchucks live in a den five or six feet below the surface. Storms may come and go, but the woodchuck sleeps till the first flowers wake. The grizzly and black bear spend from three to five months in heavy, hibernating sleep.

Plants, too, though anchored, have a variety of winter customs. Trees may be said to hibernate, even the firs and spruces that go to sleep in full dress. Beneath the snow are countless seeds that will live their life next year, and numbers of plants that have hauled down their towers and colors for the winter. You may seek them and walk over them, and Mother Nature will only say: "Trouble me not, for the door is now shut and my children are with me in bed."

Moss in midwinter is as fresh and charming as though knee-deep in June. It is dainty and striking in a white setting. Mosses and lichens are ever a part of the poetry associated with ferns and the golden sands of bubbling springs; they are sharers in the cheerful, ever-silent beauty of the wild. They never intrude, but are among the most subdued and harmonious decorations in all nature. Yet lichens carry all the colors of the rainbow. In dark woods, deep canyons, and on the pinnacles of high peaks they cling in leafy, maplike decoration of oxidized silver, hammered brass, pure copper, and stains of yellow, brown, scarlet, gray, and green. They are almost classical decorations and touch with soft color and beauty the roughest bark and boulders. Until one knows that they are living things they seem only chemical colorings on the crags, and a part of the color scheme in the bark of trees.

One day during this outing I had been walking in the shadow of a mountain, which, together with the darkness of the spruce

Enos A. Mills on a snowy summit in the Rockies.

woods, made the snow almost a gray expanse. As I climbed out of the shadow on to a plateau, just at sunset, how splendidly, dazzlingly white was the skyline of peaks! On this white and broken line the sunset-colored clouds strangely rested. A sunset is never an old story, and a colored sunset above the white west line of winter's silent earth renews the imagination of youth.

Though I crossed a number of alpine lakes they were not to be seen. They were gone from the landscape. A stratum of marble instead of snow could not better have concealed them. Lakes, flowers, and bears were asleep for the winter.

In snowless places the brooks had decorated their ways with beautiful ice structures—arches and arcades, spires and frozen splashes, and endless stretches and forms of silver streamside platings and boulder drapings; ice, crystal clear, frosted and opaque. Many rocks were overspread with ice sheets and icy drapery, and cliffs were decked with fretwork and stupendous icicles. Smaller streams froze to the bottom, overflowed and outbuilt. In places wide areas were covered to enormous depths. Looking upon these one might almost fancy the Ice Age returning. Three months later the ice was gone to the far-off sea, and the flowers that slept beneath were massing their brilliant blossoms in the sun.

An old Ute chief once told me that during the hardest winter he had ever known in his country the snow for weeks lay "six ponies deep." The average annual snowfall in the Rocky Mountains is less than twenty-five feet. This is less than the average for the Alps.

Meetings with other human beings were few. One day, while walking down a plateau, I saw a dark figure that stood waiting on the edge of a snowy mountain moor a mile distant. As I approached the man waved an arm to attract my attention and when I came near enough he said by way of greeting:

"I thought you had not seen me."

We were above the limits of tree growth, and below and about us was a wild array of peaks and canyons.

"When I saw you come racing down that peak shoulder," said the man, "I fancied that you were an escaping Siberian convict, sentenced for political aims. What is your sentence or your service?"

"They call me the Snow Man," I replied. "I am making winter experiments and gathering information along the summit of the Continental Divide." I had not as yet become official "Colorado Snow Observer."

In answer to a counter question of mine he said:

"Oh, I'm a prospector, fifty-four, born in Ireland, raised in Australia and Siberia. Am after gold in Spruce Gulch. If I don't strike it by spring I'm off for Alaska. Stirring reports from there."

It was a good place to look around. Several towering peaks were strangely near. A number of summits reached up fourteen thousand feet into the blue sky. Colorado is crowded with a vast and wondrous array of mountains. Many of these are united by narrow plateaus that are savagely side-cut with deep canyons. Each time I gained a commanding height I looked again and again, awed by the immensity of it all, at peaks and canyons with their broken strata of snow.

This outing, as usual, was all too short. Ten of its fourteen days were sunny and calm. Through two days the wind roared. Two other days were filled with snowstorms. Each day I went to some new scene. I climbed one fourteen-thousand-foot peak. I occupied one camp three nights, but on each of the other nights I had a new camp. Most of the nights were filled with stars, and always there was the blazing campfire. On my way home I met a man who had heard of my winter camping habits. After questioning me concerning the objects of interest seen, he asked:

"Is this a good time of year for a vacation?"

I replied:

"A good time for a vacation is whenever you can spare the time, and the very best time for a vacation in the mountains is when you can stay the longest."

At left: Elizabeth Frayer Burnell guides on Long's Peak.

Below: Elizabeth Frayer Burnell in Wild Basin, Long's Peak in the background.

Poor naked wretches, whereso'er you are,
That bide the pelting of this pitiless storm,
How shall your houseless heads and unfed sides,
Your loop'd and window'd raggedness, defend you
From seasons such as these?
                                    —Shakespeare.

Trees at Timberline

All day I followed the dwarfed, battered, uppermost edge of the forest through the heights of the Rockies. My barometer steadily said that we were two miles higher than the sea. From a stand of dead timber I cut eleven small trees and carried them in one load to my campfire. They were so gnarled and ancient looking that they aroused my curiosity, and with a magnifier I counted the annual rings in each. The youngest was 146 years of age, and the oldest 258! The total age of these eleven trees was 2,191 years! These and other trees had blazed in my fire and fallen to ashes long before I fell to sleep beneath the low and crowded stars.

With rare exceptions the trees at timberline are undersized and of imperfect form. A forest only eight feet high is not uncommon. One winter a tough staff that I used was almost an entire tree which had been nearly 400 years in growing. A tree that I carried home in my pocket the microscope showed to be more than three score and ten years old! Annual rings in many of these timberline trees are scarcely 1-100 of an inch in diameter, while a fate-favored cottonwood or eucalyptus may in one season envelop itself with a ring that is more than an inch in diameter.

The age of a timberline tree cannot be approximated by its size or appearance or by the size or the age of its neighbors. It may have lived twice as long, and it may have endured more hardships than its nearby fellows of similar size and appearance.

Environment has shaped many timberline trees into huge and crooked vines. Still others are picturesque, bell-shaped individuals formed by the deeply drifting snows pressing the limbs downward and against the trunk. During the summer months the limbs partly regain their natural position, and the result is a slender bell shape in tall trees and a heavy bell outline in stocky ones. Instead of symmetrical limb development many trees are one-sided. Imagine a tree with storm-threshed limbs all flung out on one side of the trunk, like a tattered, wind-blown banner! Then imagine thousands of bannered trees scattered and grouped, in a mountainside forest front!

The climatic conditions at the forest frontier are trying, but timberline trees are hardy and probably have as long or even longer lives than the majority of their more fortunately placed relatives. The oldest timberline settler that I ever studied had been permanently located at an altitude of 11,437 feet for 1,182 years when finally killed by fire. Much-branched and stocky, its height was twelve feet, and its diameter a foot above the earth was four feet six inches. What these timberline trees lack in symmetry and heroic size they make up in hardiness and aggressiveness.

Timberland in the far northland marks the latitudinal limits, while the mountain timberline shows the altitudinal limits of the forest life zone. The forest farthest north ends in a ragged, battered edge against the Arctic prairies. The polar storms that sweep across broken ice fields and barren lands meet with first resistance in the advanced, low-crouching timberline of sturdy spruces.

Timberline far up the sides of high mountains is as strange and as abrupt a boundary as the crooked and irregular shoreline of the sea. This mountainside timberline is the forest's uppermost edge. Above are the treeless distances and barren heights of the Arctic-alpine zone. Below and away from the ragged edge drapes and rolls the dark and broken robe of forest. Like old ocean's shifting and disputed boundary line, timberline is a place where contending forces ever surge and roar.

Nowhere does this forest frontier—the ever-contending line of battle between woods and weather—appear more stormy or striking than in the high mountains of the West. For miles this timberline extends away in a front of dwarfed and distorted trees—millions of them—ever fiercely fighting a relentless enemy.

Enos A. Mills and his daughter, Enda, in a twisted pine
near timberline on the slope of Long's Peak.

The veterans show the intense severity of the struggle as they
stand resolutely in their inhospitable heights.

Timberline trees are among the distinct attractions of our
national parks. Timberline is probably the most telling in the
Rocky Mountain National Park, but in the Yosemite, Mount
Rainier, and Glacier National parks it has striking phases. It is an
illustrated and graphic story—one of the most powerful in the
book of Nature.

In Colorado this mountainside tree line is two vertical miles
above the shoreline of the sea. Like the ocean's edge, timberline
has miles that are straight and level as a die; but in places it sweeps
outward around a peninsula and follows the crooked line of an
invading canyon. There are forested bays, beautiful coves, and
wooded islands. Stretches of forest climb high ridges, and invading
outposts made a successful stand in favorable spots among the

snowfields far above the main forest front.

Violent, dry winds that blow ever from the same quarter are a powerful, relentless foe of many a forest frontier. They either point all limbs toward the leeward or prevent all limbs except leeward ones from growing. Trees are pushed out of plumb and entire forests are pushed partly over. Then overweighted with snow, they are forced down to earth and flattened out. The wind and snow never allow them to rise again, and they become in effect huge vines or low, long-bodied, prehistoric animals headed to the leeward. They refuse to die, and may live on for centuries.

Snow, cold, and dryness are the chief factors which determine where the forest may or shall not grow. In some localities the snow line is the barrier that forms the timberline. Dryness of locality combined with dry winds resists forestation. The sand blasts of dry, windy localities play havoc by beating and flaying the trees. This sand beats off the bark on the trees' stormward quarter, exposing their very bones. Often it eats its way into the already half-flayed trunks. The stormward half of many trees is dead and lifeless, a sand-graven totem pole, while the living half holds long, tattered limbs streaming leeward.

This gale-blown sand frequently prevents trees from growing higher than the shelter behind which they stand. In places so-called trees may be seen with trunks one to three feet in diameter and only one or two feet high, cut off by the sand fire of the high winds. Numerous long limbs reach out from the trunk in all directions. The shoots which these limbs send up are clipped off by the wind shot sand. In time this treetop is a table or brush of bristles twenty feet across, and trimmed off as level as a lawn. Hundreds of these trees are often crowded together until the identity of each is lost, forming acres of clipped, low tree lawn. The wide-spreading mass is too low to crawl under and not quite strong enough to allow one to walk on the surface. It is a good mattress to sleep on; often I have rolled out of one of these treetop beds without discovering the tumble till morning!

Snowslides, landslides, and other factors often pile up embankments of debris, and these form large windbreaks whose shelter allows trees to grow in places formerly windswept and inhospitable. Trees at timberline are eternally vigilant and promptly seize every new opportunity or opening. One spring a landslide on the slope of Mt. Clarence King piled a shipload of stones on a wind-swept, treeless flat. A few years later several dozen spruce were growing up in the leeward of this chance-made shelter.

Slides or other forces occasionally remove shelters behind which a forest front was formed. Or they place an obstruction which changes the course of the prevailing winds. Snowslides occasionally cut an avenue down into a forest, which exposes the trees on the edges of the new avenue. Or an old stretch of forest front is sheared off by a slide. With the hardened front ranks removed, the less hardy trees thus exposed are slashed and shot to pieces by the cutting edges of the prevailing gales.

One day I came out upon a long, hedge-like growth of trees extending down the slope. Here the high, sand-flinging winds blew from west to east. A lone boulder about six feet in diameter at the west end of the hedge had sheltered the first tree that had grown up to the leeward of it. Then another tree had risen in the shelter of this one, and still others in order and in line eastward, until the long hedge was grown. The straight line of the hedge from west to east showed that the high winds were always from the same quarter, and the topography of the place had compelled them to rush along the straight line which they had followed. The front of this hedge was the diameter of the boulder, and the farther end, about two hundred feet away, was about a foot higher. Each summer thousands of shoots and twigs grew out on the top and sides, but each succeeding winter the winds trimmed them off. Long afterward, in pursuit of a woodchuck one day, a grizzly dug out a few tons of earth and stones by the side of this boulder. Frost and water undermined, until gravity caused the boulder to roll over. The hedgerow was quickly sandblasted to pieces, and in a few years all that remained was a number of stubby trunks, half round, with the flattened, stormward side fantastically ground and engraved by the wind and sand.

I have followed the timberline for hundreds of miles, in the Sierras, the Cascades, and the Rocky Mountains. One evening I camped on the rim of Wild Basin in what is now the Rocky

Mountain National Park. Out of the opposite side off the Basin, Long's Peak swept ruggedly far up into the sky. I was on the eastern slope of the Continental Divide. Great light bars, miles in length, and long shadow pennants of peaks lay across the basin. As the sun descended, these lengthened and pushed down the descending slopes. Finally they reached out upon the Great Plains nearly a hundred miles distant. Nearby a solitaire sang with inspiring and unrivalled eloquence. He sang from a crag and from a treetop, and then with intense ecstacy, while darting and dropping, wheeling and gliding, he gladdened the air above his nesting mate. Once he rose high above the shadows and for a moment poured forth his song in the bright sunlight above.

As he ceased, the beavers began making merry in a pond just below. I watched them and the purple ripples they made. Presently the ripples faded from sight, but in the darkness the easy movements and dividing wavelets of the swimmers were revealed by the rocking of the reflected stars.

In the night a white-crowned sparrow repeatedly sang briefly. A camp-bird quietly waited for my awakening. Later a tiny chipmunk bashfully called. An astonished squirrel first stared in silence, then with jerky note scolded and bluffed from a safety-first distance, but at last gave way to curiosity and came closer.

Big game is common along the boundary of woodland and grassland. Deer and elk frequent timberline during the summer, and mountain sheep may be seen at any time. In the autumn it is frequented by bears. The mountain lion, coyote and fox come to this edge of the woods to watch and wait, and here concealed gaze out upon the upland open.

Beautiful lakes, gouged by glaciers out of solid rock, are scattered along the farthest edge of the forest. They are one of the distinctive charms of these Arctic gardens. With a border of wild cliff, a waterfall, a fringe of brilliant flowers, grassy spaces, picturesque trees in clusters and singly, these lakes are wildly, poetically lovely.

On the whole, the heights are becoming dryer. Many summits are no longer tolerant to the trees. Parts of the Rocky Mountains are in the arid belt, and their winters are often extremely dry. Dry, high winds frequently sweep their summits, sucking moisture from all vegetation. The unprotected trees in the forest front of dry ridges suffer greatly, thousands perishing during a single dry winter.

I walked for hours along a dry summit slope strewn with the bleaching bones of millions of veteran pines and spruces. Here over a long front the battle had gone against the forest. The nearest frontier was half a mile down the slope.

Timberline is not fixed. In places it is creeping forward and upward; in other reaches its is being driven back. Still other boundary lines, like those of nations, are stationary for years, then suddenly these are obliterated and redrawn, as territory is lost or won.

Only a few of the earth's numerous tree people dwell at timberline. Those most commonly found both at timberline in the heights and the low levels of the north are pine, spruce, fir, aspen, birch, and willow. On the eastern slope of Long's Peak timberline is approximately two miles above sea level. Here, in a moist place by a tiny tributary of the Mississippi, grow Engelmann spruce, Alpine fir, black birch, aspen, and Arctic willow. On a nearby dry slope all the trees are limber pines.

Elizabeth Frayer Burnell with two other women
under a twisted pine.

On Mount Orizaba, close to the equator, timberline is maintained above the altitude of 13,000 feet. In the Rockies of Colorado and in the Sierras it is at approximately 11,500 feet. The highest timberline of normal trees in the United States that I have found is on a gulch of the San Juan Mountains at an altitude of 12,300 feet. Here are upright trees more than a foot in diameter and 60 feet high. Timberline in Switzerland is about 6,500 feet; on Mount Washington about 5,000; on Mount Rainier about 7,000. In most localities it is higher on the southerly mountain slopes that on the northerly. In the far north the altitudinal and latitudinal timberlines converge and form the defensive outpost of the forest on the edge of the polar world.

Broken wildflower gardens crowd and color every ragged opening among the picturesque tree groups on the forest frontier. Many of these flowers are dwarfed and tiny but in moist places they grow thickly and tall. Among the last trees I have seen wild sheep wading shoulder deep through wide meadows of colored bloom.

A typical timberline garden is a ragged-edged acre fenced off and sheltered by a weird, low wall of trees. Here and there a blooming open way connects it with an adjoining garden. A young tree clump and a boulder pile add artistic touches; here and there appear low-growing, many-tinted phlox; tall, stately columbines with silver and blue ribbons at the top; blue mertensia, taller still; paint brushes touched with a variety of shades; anemones; gentians; white monkshood; and, bending upon its stem, a ray-faced, golden-brown gaillardia.

One winter the snow drifted deeply over a stretch of forest as large as a huge circus tent. The following summer it partly melted. The next winter new snow was added, and the following spring the drift was larger than before. It did not melt away until the third summer. In the meantime, the several hundred spruce trees were kept asleep in a natural cold storage and had failed to grow. This is why their annual rings were two less in number than those of the neighboring trees of the same age.

Trees have tongues. They record in their annual rings the larger experiences of the years, the triumphs of friendly seasons, and the batterings and the burns that fall to the lot of those in the front ranks of high mountain forests. A timberline veteran might tell of the wealth of moonlight on a winter night, with forest outposts half buried in the white snow; of crowded stars in the field of space; of terrific winds and irresistible avalanches of vast snow piles.

With flying snow, in perfect autumn days and during mist-filled nights, I have slept and communed with my campfire at timberline. Timberline gives one the feeling of being on the edge of things. Envelop it in unevenly moving mist and everything seems a mystery. The strangely shaped trees and the weird forms of tree clumps half revealed are a part of the indefinite, the uncomprehended. Add to this vague realm the magic of a campfire, and one loses the experience of ages and again is a primitive, crouching fire worshipper in a new and unexplored world. A campfire ever recalls the ages long past, and paints primeval scenes. Through all the centuries the campfire has been a place of safety and comfort, of hope and cheer.

Though they stand in one place all their years, trees have adventurous lives from their seedling days to battered old age, and stored in their unrolled and untranslated annual rings are their records and perhaps glimpses of the everchanging scenes in which they grew. Sometimes while watching my changing campfire blaze I have half believed that the blazing tree was picturing with fire the story of its life—the larger experiences of the years; the triumphs of the good seasons and the failures of the bad; the battles with wind and frost, with fire and insect foes. Surely no picture ever painted is more suggestive than the campfire. With it the imagination brings the dead past back to life, and its people in fitting scenes act again the parts they once played.

The Big Trees of California are the greatest living wonders of the world. In the serene Sierras they have achieved the dignity befitting the largest and the oldest living things upon this earth. Compared with these Big Trees the timberline trees of the Rockies are pygmies and infants. Yet who shall say that the life story of the timberline tree is the less inspiring. To stand beneath the Big Trees is to feel the silent eloquence of the "noblest of a noble race." To stand above the dwarfed and battered front ranks of the intrepid timberline forests, where the Storm King reigns and the eagle soars, is to live with fired imagination through all the long years of battle, and to feel the triumphs of the unconquerable. Timberline touches the heart with a sense of universal kinship.

Enos A. Mills beside a twisted pine near timberline.

Life is a daring adventure...or nothing.
                                    —Helen Keller.

Wind-Rapids on the Heights

Terrific winter winds occasionally sweep through the high passes of the Continental Divide. Believing that their velocity was sometimes more than one hundred miles an hour, I planned to go up and measure the velocity of the next wind that appeared to be exceeding the speed limit. An air meter was placed in Granite Pass. This was on the Long's Peak trail, about one mile beyond the limits of tree growth and at an elevation of more than two miles above the level of the sea.

One February morning the rush and boom of the wind among the pines proclaimed that previous speed records were likely to be broken. I left my cabin and started up to the meter, which was about three thousand feet higher than my cabin and five miles from it.

In irregular succession the heavy waves of wind rolled down this slope into the forest. A splendid and stormy sea roared through the treetops. The first half mile was through a thicket growth of tall young pines. These young and pliant trees were bending, shaking, and streaming in the wind. I turned aside from the trail to see the behavior of the tallest woods, a dense growth of Engelmann spruce, at the bottom of the steep slope of Battle Mountain.

I climbed into a treetop one hundred feet high. Around me the tall and crowded trees were swaying and bowing through a dignified dance. Invisible wind breakers produced sudden dips and vigorous sweeps that my old tree thought he enjoyed. Occasionally the treetop swayed in one direction, then bowed in another. Once he nodded in succession toward all points of the compass, tracing a wavy circle perhaps twenty feet in diameter. Then he straightened up again to the perpendicular. The entire forest was suddenly tilted forward by a violent wind wave and without the least warning I was clinging to a leaning tower. Engelmann spruce wood is not celebrated for toughness so I quickly descended to earth.

In the shelter of the storm-battered trees at timberline I looked out into the yellow, sand-filled air upon a treeless Arctic moorland. The gale tore among the trees with ever-varying intensity. Sand and gravel pattered and rattled against the scarred and veteran pines. I climbed a low, stocky tree which the hardest wind waves struck. This tree was so rigid that it quivered and oscillated like a building in an earthquake.

At the altitude of 11,500 feet I emerged from the woods and faced the gale. It assailed me with a sand blast which bruised my hands and brought blood from my face, and speedily drove me back into the woods. Again I tried. This time I crawled forward between low, healthy growths. At the start these afforded a little protection but as I advanced the wind swept through more swiftly and violently. I was glad to crawl out into the open moorland. Here, after an advance of a few hundred yards, I paused to rest in the lee of a butte of granite. Thicker than hail the sand and gravel rained down upon me; a roll of my coat caught a handful. Much of this consisted of sand-bits the size of a pencil point, but there were a few pieces of gravel the size of hazel nuts; the remainder was rock dust crushed by colliding with the cliff.

It was a warm, dry, chinook wind. Its temperature was several degrees above the freezing point. There had been but little snow, and only a few small, icy drifts lay scattered upon the brown, bare moor. The sun shone in a cloudless sky, but the air was so filled with rock dust that objects more than one hundred feet away were out of focus in the hazy yellow air. The effect was that of a desert sand storm; the wind, however, was of greater velocity and carried less dust than in desert storms.

Leaving the shelter of the cliff, I again advanced by crawling. A brief stop was made behind a rock point about five feet high. Here the wind poured down upon me with such force that it could not be endured.

Thus far above the limits of the trees not a living thing had showed itself, but in crawling along the edge of an icy snowdrift I came upon a number of ptarmigan. Many were sitting in little nests just the size of their bodies, which they had made in the hard snow. A few were bravely feeding. Squatting low, they grabbed at weed seeds and other edible objects that came sifting down over the snow. Though in a sheltered place, one of them was occasionally bowled over by the wind. On regaining its feet, it struggled back into its nest. Not one risked opening its wings. Apparently they considered me as harmless as a mountain sheep. With curious eyes, they allowed me to crawl by within three feet.

The wind met me with violent dashes, with moderate movements, and with occasional intervals that were almost calm. In many of its rushes the wind rolled forward like a stormy breaker, with invisible, unbroken wave front in a sustained roar. At other times, this great wave was broken into wild maelstroms, terrific spirals of various diameters and tilted at every angle. Sometimes a wave went forward with long, bouncing leaps, bounding entirely clear of the earth for long distances, then striking heavily to roll and break, like a breaker on the beach. Occasionally, over a small space, there was an explosive effect that sent dust and gravel flying. With slouch hat and mittened hands I protected my face as best I could. A few times a violent, narrow whirlwind cut unrestrained into unrelated air currents. Like the explosion of a cannon and by sheer speed and force, it smashed its way diagonally across and through other rushing winds.

Most of the time I crawled, but occasionally during a calm I rose up and ran forward a few hundred feet. Except during lulls it was perilous to stand erect. These winds could not be withstood by bracing. Main strength did not answer. Rarely did they strike straight forward; they struck on every side. Seldom was I blown over, but I was kicked into the air and I was sometimes knocked down or hurled to one side.

At last I gained the air meter. It was up at 12,000 feet and stood where the wind simply pounded through the pass. The meter cups were making a blurred wheel of speed; a few times they showed the wind at one hundred and seventy miles an hour.

Around me were high peaks and deep canyons, level plateaus and crag-torn slopes. These intercepted and deflected the wind waves and currents. Against these obstructions the powerful, invisible wind hurled itself more uproariously than storm-stirred sea against defying and moveless shore.

Ever from some quarter came an unending roar. Splendid were the deep sounds and thunderings, ponderously heavy and prolonged were the booms of the wind. These often mingled with terrific, crashing explosions which even the elastic air did not always soften. There were long, ripping sounds, as the diverted wind rolled up a slope or tore around a corner. Then, strange were the seconds of ominous, almost breathless, calm.

After reading the meter, I went higher. Carried away with the wild, elemental eloquence of the storm, I concluded to get effects from the high ledges and finally from the summit of Long's Peak.

Every step advanced, each new height somehow gained, was a fight. It took all my endurance and it stimulated utmost alertness. I simply crawled forward and upward. And I wrestled with an invisible, unresting contestant who occasionally tried to hurl me over a ledge or smash my bones against the rocks.

For a mile I made my way across a moraine with the wind beating against my right side. The scattered boulders made traveling difficult; many were large and had to be climbed over. Such activities often gave the wind the eagerly used opportunity of shooting me with icy pellets and of knocking me off my feet.

Sand-blasted limber pines near timberline.

At the altitude of thirteen thousand feet, the trail was through a rocky opening called Keyhole. Here the wind rushed in an invisible but irresistible flood. To go against it was sheer madness, so I climbed down and around Keyhole. While doing this, as I lay flat on my face, I was caught by a rush of wind. It lifted me a foot or two, then jammed me back. After repeating this, it pitched me headlong!

The wind swept out of the west and came in contact with the Divide at right angles. On the east the wind blew everywhere; but strangely enough on the western side it struck the mountains from eleven thousand feet upward, below this was perfect calm. By watching the whirling snow and other windblown materials, I judged this wind current to be about two thousand feet thick. Above, approximately thirteen thousand feet, was an air current moving in nearly the opposite direction. In crossing the Divide this wind that was blowing high above the earth on the west side closely raked the earth on the eastern side. From points near the top of the Peak I looked out over my home to the east. Two thousand feet above it the air was comparatively free from dust. To the east I saw a number of birds flying high and plainly in a calm stratum of air.

As I continued upward above thirteen thousand feet, the wind gushed and stormed through the narrow openings between pinnacles and around the large rocks in debris piles. I crawled through a number of these openings. There are rapids in rivers and rapids in air streams. Running a river rapid in a boat is exhilarating. Crawling through a wind rapid is even more intense. It lacks most of the exhilaration that goes with the river rapid, but exhilaration is not wholly absent. In bays and channels of the sea the restless waters wildly eddy; powerful, invisible undertows and whirlpools are present where wild, defiant winds are diverted.

Rock projections, behind which I hoped to find shelter, were more unfriendly places than the open. The wind appeared to round them with increased speed, and to batter the leeward more furiously than the stormward front. Around a number of rocky projections the wind revolved with swirling rapidity. It hurled me off with centrifugal motion each time I made close approach.

Once I blundered by breaking into one of these whirls, and was roughly handled while in and while getting out of it.

Each time that I hugged the earth more closely than usual, the wind took a sheer delight in paying me personal attentions. While many of these calls were with evil intentions, the others were but the investigations of the curious. I was grabbed and then slammed back; I was trampled upon and several times was recklessly dragged over rough stones. I was occasionally raised gently upward, then laid gently down; rolled slowly over, then turned slowly back. Once I was picked carefully up by a current that carried me off as carefully as if to first aid; but from this I was rudely snatched by an angry wind, whose every effort was to put me in need of this aid.

The most difficult and dangerous place was at a point at an altitude of about fourteen thousand feet. This was where a long, narrow gulch and a fan-like slope converged and ended on the summit of a narrow ridge, beyond which there was a narrow ledge, bounded by unbanistered space. Sweeping upward three thousand feet from the bottom of a canyon came the wind through converging channels that ended in this one narrow gorge. My struggles were intense in the last few feet of this channel. The gorge in which I climbed was extremely steep, yet so powerful was the wind current that all my strength was required to prevent being torn loose, shot upward, and thrown over the precipice. Icy fragments torn from the walls, twigs from a mile below, went hurtling and rattling by and shot far out over the precipice. Had I let go for even a second, I should have followed them. Not for an instant did the wind stop; it had the constant rush of rapids. I eased myself upward in the rushing wind, crawling close, holding with hands, and anchoring and holding rear down by hooking feet behind and beneath rocks. Trail conditions were favorable, and these together with my climbing experiences, endurance, and knowledge of the place, were of advantage to me. All these were needed.

Just before reaching the top of the narrow ridge and the precipice, I felt the wind getting the better of me and feared that a slightly more violent rush or surge would tear my holds loose. So I concluded to reverse ends. Putting a shoulder against a rock point, I allowed the wind to push my legs around, then forward. I was then going up feet foremost instead of head foremost. The gully was so extremely steep that I was almost standing or walking on my head. This reverse of ends enabled me to brace effectively with my feet, and also to hang on more securely with my hands. Little by little I eased myself upward. There was no climbing; the wind sucked, dragged, pushed, and floated me ever upward.

At last I safely crossed the ridge, rounded a point, and sat down for a long rest on the famous Narrows of the Long's Peak trail. The Narrows is a ledge with a precipice in front and a wall behind. This wall rises precipitously to the summit; the precipice makes a wild, steep descent of two thousand feet. It is none too wide for a thoroughfare that has unbanistered space before it. Fortunately, it was sheltered from the wind, otherwise traversing it would not have been either safe or sane.

Why did I, in this perilous gale, in this wild wind, venture precipices and go up into the sky on a peak nearly three miles above the seven restless seas?

Irresistible is nature's call to play. This call comes in a thousand alluring forms. It comes at unexpected times and sends us to unheard-of places. We simply cannot tell what nature will have of us, or where next. From near and far, ever calls her eloquent voice. In work and in dreams she shows a thousand ways, suggests the presence of wonderlands yet unseen. She pictures alluring scenes in which to rest and play; in mysterious ways she sends us eagerly forth for unscaled heights and fairylands. Of these she whispers, or of them she sounds her bugle song. She fascinatingly commands and charms us to other scenes. We rush to respond and fix our eyes on a happy horizon, toward which we hurry; but ere we reach it she calls elsewhere, and elsewhere, with highest hopes of a boy at play, we hasten. It was seriously splendid to play with these wild winds. There is no greater joy than wrestling naked handed with the elements.

My most uncertain work was a little below the summit. The ridge that had shielded my crawling came to an end. I was on the edge of a steep, short slope that ended at the top, but this slope was smooth and icy and at the bottom paid tribute to a precipice.

It was too slippery to climb. Across it swept the deflected wind current. On the opposite side the current struck a ridge and with diminished force shot upward to the summit. Apparently this wind rushed as steadily as a mountain river. It was swift enough to sweep me across; but if it hesitated after I cast my lot in it, down the toboggan slope I would slide. Eagerly I pushed myself out into it and let go. Across it rushed me, sprawling, bumping me into the rocky ridge beyond. Here the interrupted current lifted me upward. I had little else to do than guide myself. Rapidly it boosted to the top. Standing on the edge of the summit I turned for a moment to look back down this icy slope which later I must somehow retrace.

The summit of Long's Peak is 14,255 feet above the sea and about four hundred feet in diameter. It is comparatively level though not smooth. Granite stones and slabs of various sizes cover the top.

In terrific, weighty rushes the wind splendidly thundered against the west wall of the summit. All this time the wind was continuously roaring round lower pinnacles and terrifically booming against the lower obstructions. The old Peak met these cyclonic rushes with strange impassiveness, without a tremble. Deflected by the west wall, the current shot upward for a hundred feet or so. The top of the Peak was thus left in comparative calm.

I ventured too close to the west edge, and my hat was torn off. It started skyward like a rocket, but less than one hundred feet above the Peak it fell out of the uprush and into the large, slowly rotating eddy that covered the space over the top. Slowly around in a large air whirlpool the hat was carried. I threw a number of stones, trying to bring it back to earth. Presently the forward current caught it. Then like a duck in a wind the hat shot forward, pointing straight at a lower and nearby lighting place.

A flock of rosy finches were feeding off the stuff that sifted down out of the wind. As I watched them, they were unmindful of the wind and had thought of no danger. Behind a nearby stone a beady-eyed weasel watched and waited.

Far down the range to the south quantities of snow were being explosively hurled into the air. This showed that there had been a recent snowfall and also that the wind had just reached that scene. The scattered snow was thrown high in the air into spirals and whirls and then seized and carried flying to the leeward. This powdered snow trimmed the Peak points with steamy whirls and gauzy banners and silky pennants through which the sunlight played. Northward for one hundred miles the gale was sweeping eastward, and a stratum of dust hid the Wyoming plains. The sky above was clear and strangely blue. The sun shone brightly. My shadow against a granite monolith stood out as if of a dark and sculptured figure cut from stone.

Trees near timberline in the high winds on the heights of the Rockies.

The woods were made for the hunters of dreams,
The brooks for the fishers of song;
To the hunters who hunt for the gunless game
The streams and the woods belong.
There are thoughts that moan from the soul of a pine,
And thoughts in the flower bell curled;
And the thoughts that are blown with the scent of the fern
Are as new and as old as the world.
                                          —Sam Walter Foss

The Arctic Zone of High Mountains

The peaks and plateaus of high mountains are distinguished by a climatic zone that is somewhat similar to that of Arctic regions. Many species of plants and birds of polar zones are found in the broken summit lands of the Rocky Mountains, the Sierras, and other high-lifted mountains. The Alps, the summit slopes of the Himalayas and other Asiatic mountains, those of Mexico and the Andes, all carry their own characteristic Arctic gardens.

Mount Washington, and a few of the peaks of New England and New York, and numbers of the peaks in national parks carry luxuriant wild Arctic gardens on their high-held heads and shoulders. On Mount Rainier, between the timberline and the snow line, there is perhaps the greatest wild garden in the world. A great, brilliantly colored wreath a mile wide and fifty miles in circumference encircles the peak, touched here and there with glaciers. On Mount McKinley, between three thousand and seven thousand feet above the sea, is another splendid and magnificent garden filled with wild flowers and wild life.

In the Colorado Rockies the Arctic outpost that lies above the timberline embraces about five million acres. It has more than one thousand peaks. These sky-held, island-like areas, more than two miles above the sea, are less known than islands of the South Sea. They carry lakes, canyons, tundras, moorlands, snowfields, and many a lichen-tinted cliff and rock slide.

This mountain plateau region of the Rockies which lies

The Narrows, Long's Peak, in winter.

between the peak summits and the timberline is a world by itself. It has its storms and its moving wreaths and strata of clouds, and also its full share of sunshine. It carries rare scenery, and its countless outlying rims and edges, where the plateaus of the sky break off and steeply descend into lakes, canyons, and mountain valleys, are scene-commanding viewpoints; these are close to the stars, show the forests and streams, the lights and shadows below and the sunset clouds on the nearby horizons of the sky.

Brilliant wild flowers enrich the treeless prairies and the grassy, sedgy meadows. Many are dwarfed to tiny smallness but others grow with even greater than lowland vigor. Their colors are varied and brilliant and many are perfumed.

In these sky lands numerous birds nest and sing; here bears and woodchucks roam; grasshoppers leap and fan their wings, and butterflies float in painted glory.

It is the home of the Bighorn and the cony; the ptarmigan and the rosy finch, too, enjoy this realm throughout the year. The summer visitors are also happy: deer, elk, coyotes, southland birds, and eagles all make merry on its peaks and moorlands. So, too, do the flocks of birds of many species from lowlands and far north who briefly visit it during the early autumn for picnic feasts while journeying toward winter homes somewhere under southern skies.

One of the strangest wild life gatherings that I have ever seen was in the Arctic-alpine zone of a mountain plateau twelve thousand feet above the sea. If you wish to have an experience entirely new, to see wild birds and wild animals in a happy commingling in the mountains, to witness a boisterous wild life feast and fair, then visit the realm just above the timberline in the Rocky Mountains when the birds are flying south.

No food station along the way of migrating birds can show a more motley or spectacular gathering than an autumnal one on these heights. It is often made up of flocks of migrating birds representing numerous species. They come from Alaska, from the "barren lands," the mountains of British Columbia, and the birch-margined streams of the North Woods. They are bound for winter homes and picnic lands in Texas, Mexico, Cuba, Orinoco, and Argentina.

In addition to migrating birds, there are resident birds and visitors from down the mountain slopes, birds from the Southland that have summered in the heights, and birds that have come up from near but lower territory for this autumnal feast. They gather from near and far, like folks at a fair.

Each spring most birds moved northward a few hundred or a few thousand miles. Most of them nest and summer in the scenes which their ancestors selected. As soon as the children are ready to travel they start for the Southland. As a rule, they travel by easy stages, though a number of species travel rapidly. All must have food along the way. And in the healthy places of the heights, close to the eternal snowfields—in the Arctic moorlands of the Rocky Mountains two miles above the level of the sea—many birds pause and celebrate. With this celebration they close summer, begin autumn, and anticipate the winter.

The setting for this festival is one of strange beauty and wild magnificence. The forest frontier with its scattering of dwarfed and storm-battered trees curtains this stage from the world below; storied old snow-piles are a part of the scenery; so, too, the high, near peaks; the enormous moraines; the clear brooks—glad and wild with energy, vigorously beginning a thousand-mile journey to the sea. Crags stand in healthy meadows, and huge, scattered boulders are near the low-growing Arctic willows. Leaves in the forest edge are taking on autumn color, and in the open spaces the mountainside is bright with late flowers.

In these moorlands are scattered the last and best of Nature's crop of choice berries—kinnikinick, currant, wintergreen, blueberry, and bunchberry. In the lowlands the berries have been gone for days and even weeks. One feels that Nature is taking unusual liberties in the plant world; that summer has added a postscript to her season and has climbed the mountain tops for the benefit of her feathered and furred creatures.

Arctic plants are scattering their seeds to the winds. The succulent leaves of many of the plants which farther down the mountain slope or in the valley have long since made plans for winter, are here in season and hanging on in all their early summer beauty.

With the last stand of summer—with its flowers, berries, and seeds—are grasshoppers and numerous accompanying varieties of insects that live upon the small plant growths. Butterflies also flourish in this land of much sunshine and few storms, and add their touch of beauty to the landscape. They are susceptible to the slightest change in temperature or weather, and at the first warning from cloud or wind drop to the ground and remain motionless until all is clear again.

Besides resident and migrating birds there are resident animals, and those that have climbed up from the lower slopes. These wild creatures, both great and small, are certain to find and to enjoy the rare feast that Nature spreads. This region above timberline is little visited by man, and rarely are its spectacles seen.

The Bighorn sheep—the monarch of the mountain tops—sometimes looks on at these feasts. He is at home among the crags in any season or condition of weather, and travels over the steep and rocky prominences with as little concern as though it were the most ordinary of accomplishments. Sheep often cross the paths of deer and elk who go to these heights for choice pasture, and at this season of the year it is not unusual to find both grazing in some rich upland meadow.

From an advantageous point upon an out-reaching crag, an uninvited guest at their reception, I was absorbed in watching a pair of bears that were slowly, deliberately, approaching a berry patch, when the shadow cast by a low-soaring eagle diverted my attention. The bears, apparently quite unconcerned by the eagle's invasion of their territory, proceeded to devastate the berry patch. It was evident that their work of laying up supplies for winter hibernation had begun.

White-crowned sparrows and juncos flew from the bushes, annoyed by the invading bears. Then flocks of birds, large and small, began to arrive. Within two hours I saw many of the species of bird life that I had followed with glass and camera in forest and lowland during the spring and summer months. White-crowned sparrows who had here raised their second brood were present in dozens; bluebirds, too, were numerous with the fledglings of both spring and summer; and Bohemian wax-wings had come to join in the general festivity before wandering down the earth for the winter. All made the most of this limited vacation, joining in the hilarity of the youngsters who had not yet learned to take life seriously. For with the bird children that predominated it was an adventure.

Literally thousands of birds were there; among them appear to be a hundred or two robins, flocks of rosy finches, a few home ptarmigan in their winter stockings, gluttonous magpies, boisterous Clarke's nutcrackers insisting on order which they never kept, a pair of gray jays from the seclusion of the woods on their yearly outing, and pipets crowded almost out of their own home territory. Even the grouse family was represented by downslope flocks. Here, where a sumptuous feast was spread—and there was plenty for all during the short period of celebration—birds mingled and intermingled with apparent unconcern. How different would have been their manner toward rival neighbors in any other season and place!

The ouzel had fled away along his alpine brook. He was not of the crowd. He rushed not for the feast, but held serenely aloof. Once he paused to sing. The clamor drowned his melody though he was close to me, but his throat and gestures told of song. Following and skimming the stream with every dip and bend that it made, he finally dropped with the water behind a cascade.

Merry chipmunks scampered about. Squirrels from below came in nervous haste and departed early. Their winter supplies were probably harvested nearer home. Curiosity alone made to them risk the dangers of this promiscuous gathering spot.

Each bird plainly was there for food and fun. If the truth were known, perhaps no visitor remained long. It seems not unlike a depot of supplies—an oasis in the desert; or was it also a bureau of information, and a reception? Here all species came for fare provided at a time when there were scanty pickings in regions inhabited the year round; for the young birds it was a break in the first long flight; for the old ones it offered ideal opportunities to rest—a breathing spell after the strenuous demands of raising and training the youngsters. The scenes were constantly changing, new arrivals disturbing the peace and quiet of the spectacle, or making no impression on the moving pageant, according to the nature and habits of the intruders.

And alas! More than once as I watched the banqueters some stronger, more cunning foe spring upon them from a hiding place near which they ventured, and thinned their ranks.

A mountain lion, and hawks both singly and in numbers, appeared in the course of the day. There was always a general scattering till they had taken a sure departure. Uninvited, unwelcome guests, they seemed to be the outcasts of the forest world, but all unconscious were they of the effect which their presence made upon their fellow creatures. They exhibited their natural traits of spying, prowling, and sweeping down upon their prey, which was not always successful in eluding them. And so one species fed upon another, showing the inexorable laws of Nature and the bitter struggle for existence which cannot be suspended even during a short and pleasurable trip to this beautiful world of the mountain tops. In fact, here as elsewhere, caution, cunning, and endurance were required for these wild animal folk to defend themselves in their temporary abiding place—their exotic camping ground.

For a time two coyotes lingered near, watching the scene and looking occasionally at each other as if exchanging similar ideas concerning the demonstration. One broke away and a few minutes later disappeared down in the woods. The other sat back on his haunches, and as though having forgotten his purpose, became deeply engrossed in moral reflection appropriate to the occasion.

The coyote appears to be the philosopher and the cynic of the wilds. Though ever hungry, ever seeking a feast, he seems always ready to show contempt for the duller wits of the world, and to indulge in a flow of philosophic thought concerning wild-folk habits and follies.

During a temporary calm in proceedings two deer passed not far away. They had perhaps come down from a moorland where early snows temporarily covered their grazing land. A number of Bighorn sheep, which had long been enjoying these unusual demonstrations in their stamping ground, stood gazing from a gallery of a boulder pile. They had no fear of being molested, for in a fraction of a second they could drop off the ledge and descend into the canyon in safety.

I could have watched this mixed populace of the wilderness not only for hours, but for days. What I had seen was only a small part of that wonderful transformation of the quiet, treeless realm which occurs once a year, occupying, with variations, several days. It is a strange and scenic common meeting place of bird and beast, friend and foe.

Above the Timberline

One guiding trip arouses interest in proper and fitting outing clothes

ENOS A. MILLS,
Rocky Mountain National Park,
Longs Peak, Colorado

66

To have risked so much in our efforts to mold nature to our satisfaction and yet to have failed in achieving our goal would indeed be the final irony. Yet this, it seems, is our situation.

—Rachel Carson

Naturalist Meets Prospector

No treetop adventures were in my plans when, one autumn afternoon, I started out for a three weeks' trip on the summit slopes of the Rocky Mountains. Nor was I planning to have discussions with prospectors. Their ways were not mine, nor my ways theirs; which fact, as will be seen, caused me trouble.

I thought to be in the wilds alone. I carried no firearms; just a raincoat, a few pounds of raisins, and a hatchet. Along the way I intended to visit beaver colonies, trees at timberline, alpine lakes, and glacier meadows, and hoped to extend my acquaintance with that strange tree—the lodgepole pine. I had made many similar trips and was ready as usual to delay and watch wild animals by the hour, or to turn aside and investigate any subject of interest, whether new or old.

For a while all went smoothly. A few miles from my cabin I came to a number of beaver colonies on the slope of Long's Peak. They were strung bead-like in the shallow channel of a stream along the top of a gigantic moraine that thrust forward like a great delta from a canyon. At that time it was commonly believed that winter weather could be foretold from the autumn preparations of beavers. If they raised the height of their dam and deepened the pond it meant cold weather and unusually thick ice. If they laid in an extra large food supply it meant that the winter would be long. I had assumed this theory to be correct, but on this trip I had to change my old belief in beaver weather wisdom. At one place two colonies side by side had made unlike preparations. In one, extensive and almost complete preparations had been made for the winter. In the other, the beavers had just begun to cut down trees for the winter food supply and neither house nor dam had

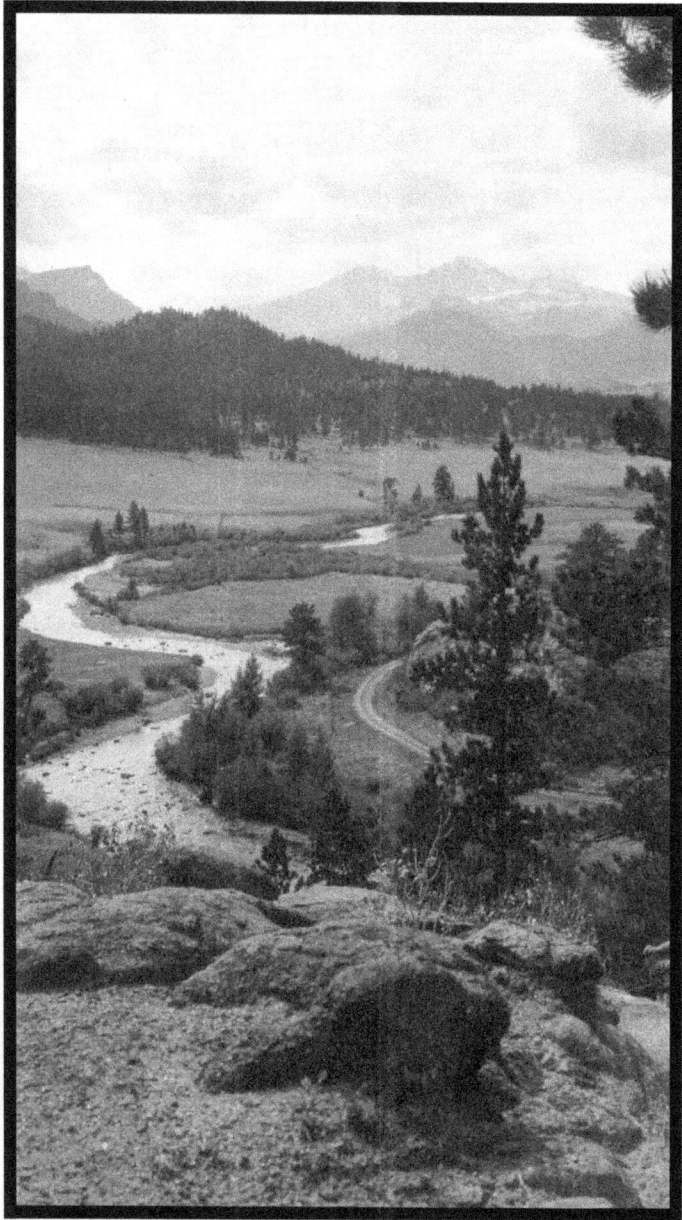

The Big Thompson River and Long's Peak.

been repaired. After I had seen many similar cases it was impressed upon me that the extent of the preparations which beavers made for winter was determined by the requirements of the colony, chiefly by the number of beavers in it. If dam or house was repaired it was because it needed repairs. Beginning these preparations early or beginning of them late might be due to the greater or less amount of work to be done, or to the individuality of the leader of a colony.

I lingered among crags in a moorland above the timberline and watched a flock of Bighorn sheep. A number were feeding, others were playing, and a few were lying down. Two sentinels, each poised upon a commanding rock, were eternally vigilant for possible danger. They appeared not to suspect a nearby enemy. On a rock cliff that cut into the sky a mountain lion crouched and occasionally raised his head. For more than an hour he lay looking down on the sheep. When the sheep started to feed away from these rocks the lion descended and disappeared.

The first treetop incident of my trip, though interesting, lacked the amusing yet annoying features of the later ones. In what is now Wild Basin in the Rocky Mountain National Park, while examining peeled places on high limbs—evidently the work of porcupines—I chanced to look across a small nearby opening and saw a little black bear ambling along. He walked up to a limber pine and climbed into it. Three limbs that outshot from the trunk about thirty feet above the earth afforded a resting place and he lay down upon his back and apparently at once went to sleep. Black bears may almost be considered perching animals, for much of the time when not active they rest or sleep in a treetop. Each bear appears to have one or more trees in his territory that he regularly uses.

Then began my adventures.

In the neighborhood of Arapaho Peak I climbed into another treetop hoping to discover the cause of the tree's dying condition. Climbing outward on a huge, steeply inclined limb, I hugged it closely and from time to time stopped to look carefully into the crevices in the broken bark. A stockman was concealed behind a tree clump a short distance away, watching me. He was quite unable to understand why an unarmed person should be prowling through the woods miles from anywhere; and why anyone should climb into a tree and examine it so minutely was beyond his comprehension. His astonishment knew no bounds when I descended and rapidly removed earthy matter from the roots so as to examine them.

From this treetop I had seen and decided to examine a tall spruce which appeared to be dying from a beetle attack, and I hoped to discover the species of insect that was doing the damage. Toward this tree I walked rapidly, and hurriedly climbed up into it. The stockman's curiosity got the better of him. He made haste to follow me and reached the bottom of the tree about the time I had gained the limb entanglement in the top. Throwing up a club to attract my attention, he demanded: "Which one of the monkey families are you a member of, anyway?"

I descended to have a talk with him. My explanation of nature study as the motive for the strange actions he had witnessed was accepted, evidently, with the proverbial grain of salt. As I appeared harmless he let the matter pass and told me something of himself. Droughty conditions on the plains had led him to drive his small herd of cattle into the mountains where there was luxuriant feed in a number of adjacent meadows. The stockman had a cabin nearby. As for a number of days I had been living on bark and berries, I gladly accepted his invitation and went over to supper.

He was born in Texas, had been a cowboy in that state and elsewhere in the southwest, and he entertained me mightily till midnight with stirring snatches of biography. Then I bade him goodnight, went back to my old raincoat, crawled into it, built a fire, and lay down to sleep.

We had parted the best of friends, but in the night a wolf played me a shabby trick. He raided the stockman's sparsely populated hen-roost and carried off a chicken, which he stopped to devour close to my camp. A few telltale feathers were left. The following day the stockman called my attention to them and warned me that it would not be well for me to take another chicken.

I protested my innocence, but appearances were against me. "Here you are," he said, "without a piece of bacon or a scrap of food of any kind. You don't have a gun or any means of procuring food in the wilderness. You have no visible means of support, not even your next meal is in sight. Men are often hanged on less satisfactory evidence."

The next night another chicken disappeared, and the following morning I was awakened early and rather violently, confronted by a stockman and a Winchester, and told to leave the country speedily. I saw the futility of argument and quickly complied.

Arriving an hour or so later on Buchanan Pass, about eleven thousand feet above sea level, I looked back down the mountain. With the recent encounter fresh in mind, I did not wish to risk again being taken for a lunatic or a suspicious character. No one was in sight, so I stopped to examine a number of the sprawling storm-battered trees, soon be coming absorbed in their interesting features.

The place was dry and wind-swept. Most of the trees were limber pines. Along the Continental Divide the wind blows violently, sometimes for days. Many of the trees were so wind-worn that they appeared a million years old. Numbers were able to grow only a foot or so above the level of the earth. The wind's terrific sand blasts cut off every exposed leaf and twig. At one place nearly an acre was covered with low, dense tree growth. Having a low shelter to the windward the trees had grown up to the height of nearly two feet. Above this they were trimmed off almost as level as a lawn. Again and again, through countless summers, the twigs had grown up, only to be mown off the following winter by flying sand. This had resulted in a crowded, matted, spiny growth, more dense and a great deal more rigid than a hedge top that has been annually trimmed for a generation. I walked readily all over the top and only occasionally did my feet break through. What a nice spring mattress it would have made! Jumping into a treetop or falling out of it here was but a commonplace performance.

Several miles down the western slope of the mountain a number of pieces of rich gold float had recently been found. But I was not long permitted to revel in such fancies. While I was examining the little six-foot timberline forest, three prospectors appeared. They accosted me with a request for my business. I told them of my interest in these storm-shaped trees. They wanted to know what there was unusual about them. I tried to explain the great age of these trees, the forces that had dwarfed and distorted them. They asked me for a piece of bacon. I had none. They desired to know where my roll of blankets was. I told them I did not carry one. Then they wanted to know what kind of a gun I used. To find that I was unarmed was too much for them. One asked me where I came from. He was promptly answered by one of the others who expressed the conviction that I was from an insane asylum.

This was another case were explanations would avail nothing. Quickly leaving these unsympathetic fellows I crossed the mountain, descending the western slope. I stopped occasionally to examine the trees and the tree clumps and to talk here and there to an individual old spruce. Without my knowing it, the prospectors had followed me. They thought I might have located a rich mine, and my queer conduct, in their eyes, was simply a ruse to throw them off their guard.

When far down the slope I concluded to count the number of trees in about an acre of dense spruce growth. After measuring the area I paced back and forth among the trees, touching each in turn, talking to one now and then, and making many oral comments. All the time, without my suspecting it, the three prospectors lay hidden nearby watching my every move, hearing some of the things that I said, and doubtless commenting scornfully upon the show.

On this acre were 2,741 spruces. I discovered a charred pitch-pine stump in the spruce area. It was closely surrounded by spruces about two hundred years of age. The presence of this fire-colored, fire-charred stump puzzled me, for I did not then know that this region had been swept by a forest fire about two hundred years before and that the stump had received fire-preservative treatment which enabled it to endure with but little change. With my hatchet I split off a piece of the wood and drawing my magnifying glass lay down to examine it. This proceeding was too much for the prospectors. They rushed upon me, demanding to know if I had found gold, and were disgusted to see me examining a piece of pitch-pine. Their comments were so uncivil that I promptly left them and wandered away into the woods. Again, without my knowledge, they followed.

After traveling about a mile I came to a glacial meadow surrounded by an Engelmann spruce growth. In the margin between spruce and meadow I found a splendid grove of lodge-pole pines and stopped to examine them. They, too, were nearly two hundred years of age. They stood close together, and the crowding had prevented their being much more than towering poles about one hundred feet high.

The lodgepole pine lives one of the most interesting stories in all the forest world. It is a pioneer tree, to one of the first and most successful to take possession of burned-over areas. It is most easily killed by fire, yet every forest fire that sweeps its territory proves an advantage to it. Throughout the West in the last fifty years the numerous forest fires have enabled the lodgepole greatly to extend its holdings. A complete cessation of forest fires would almost exterminate it. It may be said to cooperate with fires, so closely is its life interrelated with them.

It begins to bear seeds at an early age. Often it hoards all its seeds, keeping them in the cones, and the cones on the tree, year after year, sometimes for twenty years or longer. But if a fire sweeps its territory, the wax is melted from the cones that survive; they at once open and the seeds fall out, to drop into ash-covered soil—a place where they will thrive the best. The fire has consumed insect enemies and removed the cause of shade. Most young trees will not grow without shade, but young lodgepoles will not grow in it. They thrive best in the full glare of the sun. Trees of other species that come among them and grow taller shade and exterminate them.

I was particularly drawn to one old fellow in this grove. It was without a limb for the first fifty or sixty feet and tapered so little that its trunk at the first limbs appeared to have a thickness about equal to its diameter only a few feet above the roots! This was a fraction more than twelve inches. Eager to know the diameter at the first limbs I climbed up.

Seating myself comfortably on the lowest limb, I was just in the act of measuring the trunk diameter when below I caught sight of the three approaching prospectors. Near my tree they stopped and stared up at me. Having no use for them, in fact, feeling myself above them, I paid no attention but went on measuring. Presently one called, "What in the blankety-blank are you doing up there? Come down and be blank quick about it." Down I slid.

Plainly they were greatly put out. Though I had certainly done them no harm, they seemed to consider my incomprehensible performance a personal affront, and were likely to handle me roughly. When still three or four feet above the earth I leaped from the tree, and the three heavy-booted men all kicked at me at once. They all missed me. They made a number of kicks, but being agile I managed each time to be just where their feet were not. Presently they ceased kicking and declared that I had been purposely misleading them all day. My denial did not help matters; but they finally cut short the interview by demanding that I vanish in the woods.

As this was just what I wanted to do I complied. And on the way home, unhampered by further misunderstandings of the scientific spirit, I continued my acquaintance with that interesting pioneer tree, the lodgepole pine.

Wild Basin and Long's Peak.

Sunshine is delicious, rain is refreshing, wind braces us up, snow is exhilarating; there's really no such thing as bad weather, only different kinds of good weather.

—John Ruskin

The White Cyclone

One bright winter day while snowshoeing through the San Juan Mountains I saw a snowslide make a most spectacular "run." A many-thousand-ton cliff had fallen several hundred feet upon an enormous snow and ice field. I was standing on a ridge above the timberline with peaks rising high before me when the crashing echoes warned me of what was happening.

The slide's first move was a high dive. The dislodged mass of snow, ice, and stones plunged down an extremely steep, smooth slope. Then it slid and rammed a cliff. As it went on it rammed various obstructions and finally started two other avalanches moving.

I first caught sight of the snowslide as it struck a low cliff. This contact crushed tons of snow and ice to powder. The snow dust was whirled into a gigantic geyser-like column a few hundred feet wide and more than half a mile high. It remained for several seconds the highest object in the sky, the bright sun and blue heavens behind it, then slowly disbanded.

With volume and momentum increasing as it advanced, the slide rushed downward, pursued by an enormous train of curling, whirling, snow flour and ice powder—a white cyclone. One glimpse that I had of this gravity-mad monster showed its front rapidly rolling and wildly somersaulting forward. At the bottom of the slope the slide mass must have been three hundred feet wide, half as high, and two blocks or more long.

With the momentum gained in its "run" the slide rushed a quarter of a mile up a slope which lay in its path and ascended about three hundred feet. The uphill coasting caused telescoping; a shortening in the length, a massing and enlarging of the front.

With thousands of tons of rock in its terrible front it hit a low lateral moraine at right angles, tearing an opening through the top. There was an explosion, with outflying stones and snow, and more telescoping occurred. The top of the slide plunged forward, mingling with the upward, backward-hurled front. As it struck, another splendid white dust column rolled up and lingered for a time in the sky.

In tearing through the moraine the snowslide was deflected to the left where it slid up a moderate slope. Then it curved to the right and started down grade. On the monster swept. Occasionally a section leaped high and tumbled upon the mass in front. It rounded the face of the slope, cutting a contour in the deep snow and loose stones. Finally it slid out on a level flat and after a wild coast of three miles came to a sudden standstill.

In stopping, the bottom appeared to put on brakes and drag heavily, the top to pitch forward, and the upbursting bottom to mingle with it. When it stopped it was a dark dump of convulsed snow that covered an area about three blocks long, one wide, and perhaps fifty feet deep. The wreckage was a gray, concrete-like mass of snow, earth, gravel, and stones.

One summer, a few years later, I saw the remnant of this snowslide. Most of the snow and ice had melted. Viewed from the top of the ridge across which it had rushed the remaining wreckage appeared like the ruins of a huge building in a little grassy plain. Conies and marmots had taken possession of the crumbling earth and stones.

Commonly a snowslide follows a gulch and does not race so wildly. The slide to be feared is the one that takes a new route, running amuck and smashing obstacles. The big slide described was an unusual one of this type. Such a slide may be the result of a snowdrift in a new place, may be caused by the wind blowing from an unusual quarter, or may be started by a land or rock slide or the undermining of an old snow pile.

As soon as the slide stopped I started along the wreck-strewn way over which it had run. It had traveled a crooked course and opened a ragged channel through the snow. Its widest track was nearly four hundred feet, but over the most of its meteoric course its forced passageway was less than one hundred feet wide. Off this most of the snow had been scraped. Every loose and detachable object was carried away. In spots its snout had gouged into the earth. Along the track were scattered stones and snow piles. A few places showed that the momentum of the slide had caused it to jump without touching the earth. It had leaped one ravine more than fifty feet wide.

Tons of shattered rock were swept forward, mostly in the bottom of the slide. At one point a heavy granite rock thrust up ten or twelve feet in the track. Striking this caused no perceptible check in its wild speed but there was a muffled explosion. Stones were flung from the sides and hurled through the top of the slide. Clouds of snow dust were thrown off. This contact must have thrown the internal part of the slide into fierce confusion.

In following the open way through which the main slide tore I found where this slide had started two others, one of which I heard and the other I both saw and heard. Their swift, spectacular careers and their wild, sudden endings were graphically, dramatically shown in the torn and imprinted snow. These slides were set in motion just after the main slide was well under way. Although I did not see slide number two, I heard it. Slide number three I both saw and heard.

At one point the main slide had dislodged a number of boulders. The small boulders started a miniature slide that after slipping a short distance came to a standstill. One boulder must have weighed fifty tons. This enormous fellow had gone bounding down a slope with long leaps, striking a snowdrift and a rock pile which lay at the top of a steep, glaciated incline. Down this incline plunged slide number two, gathering all the snow and stones along the way.

As the slide came into the bottom of the canyon it hit a small ice-bound lake that lay in a rocky basin, smashing the ice and sweeping out most of the water. The farther canyon wall was deluged with water which promptly froze in a rough ice sheet. The slide, however, continued on its way.

Just beyond the lake it rammed the canyon wall at an angle. Apparently it was thrown off to the right and turned upside down. Ice cakes and stones were scattered and piled in the bottom of the canyon. Torn and splashed places in the snow far up on the canyon walls showed where flying stones had struck. The slide rushed on down the gorge and after a run of nearly a mile its terrific momentum caused it to jump completely out of the gorge on the outside of a curve at a point where the wall was low. This ended its career. A high and long-enduring dust column ascended from the place where it landed.

Gravity is the pull that moves snow as well as water. Slides need a slope for their coasting. On a steep, smooth slope a comparatively small accumulation or weight of snow will slide off. But if the slope is somewhat flattened or extremely rough an enormous quantity may be required for the starting, or if the weather be warm when the first autumn snow falls it may partly melt and freeze fast. This icy cement will probably endure until spring.

Most slides follow the channels of water courses. Slides may be ordinarily divided into storm, annual, and century. A storm slide may run during or shortly after the snowstorm. The annual slide for the spring will carry most of the winter's accumulation of snow; the century, the accumulation of scores of winters. The century snow slide often does much damage by smashing its way down through forests, making as it were a right-of-way of its own. A storm slide, too, may be a dangerous and damaging one. If there is an unusual fall of snow from an uncommon quarter, or if this snow is drifted in an unusual place, it, like the century slide, will smash down over a new track and leave a line of wreckage behind it.

The third slide was also started by the first slide striking a mass of snow and stones in the upper end of a shallow ravine. For more than a mile this third slide ran on a course parallel with that of the first in a weirdly spectacular race. Then slide number three swerved and followed a crescent-shaped course to the right. A succession of short-lived snow clouds were thrown explosively off as it struck obstructions.

I caught sight of this slide just as a flock of Bighorn sheep rushed out of the snow dust on one side, like frightened people almost struck by a flying express. It is probable that one or two of the sheep were caught and carried down by the slide. As the dust cleared, two injured sheep were seen limping along far behind the others. Another flock, alarmed by the chaotic echoings, rushed upon a cliff. There, in tense and splendid poses, singly and in groups, they watched the rushing slide.

This slide ran two miles, descending about fifteen hundred feet. Most of its descent was in the first half mile, and on the last part of its run it moved slowly.

At timberline it plunged headlong over a precipice, a leap of about four hundred feet, landing upon a steep and heavily forested slope. Several thousand trees were overthrown and smashed to splinters. The striking power of this mass of snow and stones cannot be computed. The slide probably weighed about two hundred thousand tons. On striking, the flying mass was thrown forward. Stones had bounded in all directions, cutting off trees to right and left. The forest within two hundred feet from the slide's landing place was ruined by this short, terrific bombardment. A trainload of stones and many tons of earth were dropped.

A part of the slide mass ran on and smashed down through the forest, breaking off or tearing out by the roots every tree in its course. Its path was narrow, about one hundred feet. But over this width it ran through the forest for about seven hundred feet with apparently unchecked speed. At the end of this stretch it plunged into a rocky canyon, nearly filling it with spruce pulp, splinters, cord-wood, earthy, convulsed snow, and shattered stones.

There were more than two hundred annual rings in the trees wrecked here, showing that there had not been a slide at this place for two hundred years.

In looking over the debris at the bottom of the precipice I came upon the body of a grizzly bear, badly crushed. Apparently this bear had been torn from his shallow hibernating cave some-where in the track of the slide, probably a short distance above timberline. Careful search failed to reveal the body of a sheep; still there may have been a number of carcasses beneath the smashed trees and wreckage.

How quickly all this had happened! I had heard the crash, boom, and rumble and the riots of echoes, and then had seen a surprised snowfield suddenly awakened and rushing forward, wrapped in excited snow dust. Above its resting place I saw the transient, mile-high snow-dust pillar silently rise. The echoes ceased, and this dust monument quickly vanished.

Sisters Esther Burnell Mills and Elizabeth Frayer Burnell go snowshoeing.

Unless we see or hear phenomena or things from within the things themselves, we shall never succeed in recording then in our hearts.
—Matsuo Basho

Lightning and Thunder

I took shelter from a thunder storm in a prospector's cabin, far up a mountain slope. Jerry Sullivan and I stood in the open door, watching the breaking clouds over us and the drifting clouds in the canyons below, when out of an almost clear sky came a bolt lightning. It struck an aged fir tree within sixty feet of the cabin and blew it as completely to fragments as though dynamited from top to bottom. Splinters and chunks of wood were showered around us. A shattered stump two feet in diameter and not more than a foot high was all that remained of the eighty-foot fir. Booming and broken echoes of the crash resounded among the canyons.

To camouflage my feelings, I turned to Sullivan and in a matter-of-fact manner asked, "Why is it that lightning never strikes twice in the same place?"

Like lightning came the reply, "It don't need to."

However, lightning does strike twice and even repeatedly in the same place. Within one mile of my mountain home was a western yellow pine that during thirty years was struck fourteen times. It was rapped three times in a single season and twice during one storm. And is likely that it was hit a number of times during its earlier years. A scar nearly a century old just above the roots of the tree showed that one lightning stroke had burst out a chunk of wood several feet long. None of these strokes did serious damage. Many trees appear to be good conductors and rarely is one killed. This pine when finally killed by beetles was probably more than three hundred years old. Another pine, less than twenty-five feet from this one and nearly as large, was struck three times while its neighbor received fourteen strokes.

I have dissected trees in various parts of the country and occasionally found one which bore unmistakable evidences of having been struck a number of times. John Muir told me that the head of sequoia tree is sometimes struck repeatedly. He had seen living trees struck and had examined the lightning-scarred tops of fallen dead ones.

It is a common belief that lightning does not strike twice in the same place, but a colored man was convinced by appearances.

"Dat tree has been struck three times by lightnin', boss," said Sam.

"Impossible, Sam. Lightning never strikes twice in the same place, you know."

"Well, say, boss, the thing what struck it yesterday bears a strikin' 'semblance to what struck it before."

On scores of occasions during my years of camping over North America lightning appeared to see how close to me it could strike without hitting me. I once held the common and preconceived notion that there were some species of trees that lightning was pretty certain to strike, and other species which it never struck. Lightning more than any other natural agency that I know has a speedy and one hundred percent efficient way of eradicating superstitions concerning itself. The only thing certain about lightning is that there is nothing certain about it. It cannot be anticipated. It never encourages one to predict where it will strike next. It strategy is of a spectacular order and its attacks are ever a successful surprise.

Lightning strikes every known species of tree. It not only strikes trees that stand on summits but it comes down to those that lead lowly lives in canyons. There are conditions, however, which cause a tree to be frequently struck. A tall tree of any species is more likely to be rapped on the head than its contemporary of conventional height; a tree on a hill-top, being closer to the electrical field, is more likely to be struck than the tree in a ravine; a lone tree much more likely than one in a grove; in fact, the tree in a position to intercept most electrical discharges and to offer these discharges the best local the conductor into the earth is the one most likely to be struck.

In this connection it is said that trees rich in starch are much more frequently struck than those rich in rosin; that is, an elm or poplar is more likely to be hit than a pine or a spruce. Often it appears to be the tree with good current transmission that is struck. Trees deeply rooted are more frequently struck than shallow-rooted ones. If a tree is shallow-rooted, or is rooted among dry rocks, it is something of an insulator, or poor conductor. There is little likelihood of its being used by a lightning bolt in reaching the earth. A green tree rooted in a moist place or among mineralized rocks is an excellent conductor and offers shelter of first rank for those of the suicide club. The old pine struck fourteen times was rooted in an outcrop of iron ore and a number of its roots penetrated the moist soil to a nearby brook.

Years ago, while making a nature address, I was asked the question: "Does lightning ever strike a mulberry tree?" I did not know, and answered another question which was asked at the same instant, ignored the mulberry tree, and went on talking. At the next pause, however, the lady repeated her question in these words: "If I take refuge beneath a mulberry tree during a thunder storm will I be safe?" Being young, wise, and impertinent, I could not miss the opportunity to say: "Madam, it all depends upon the kind of life you're leading."

Many believe that it is most dangerous to take refuge beneath a tree during a storm, especially under a conspicuously placed tree, but as a matter of fact the majority of people struck by lightning are struck in the open fields. This risk is absurdly small. Other risks, not lightning, seriously concern life insurance companies.

There is an old proverb which is supposed to contain wisdom for those outdoors during a storm; it says, "Avoid the oak, flee from the spruce, seek the beech." This advice is obsolete. The beech receives proportionally as many raps as any other species. In the nature of things, it should be the best conductor of the three species named.

The incomplete European records concerning lightning show that members of the poplar family, aspen and cottonwood, are the species more frequently struck in that part of the world. It is quite probable that an investigation would show that these trees stand in the most inviting places or in soil that renders them an easy or even alluring conductor for lightning in its zigzag journeys from sky into earth. The most frequently struck species of tree in any locality is probably the species most numerous or in the most exposed places, or a combination of local conditions make it the superior conductor.

In western Africa is a species more frequently struck than all the other local trees. This the natives speak of as being "hated by lightning." In contrast to this expression is one which I have heard the cowboys use. In certain small zones of Arizona and New Mexico the lightning strikes with remarkable frequency, and the prevailing species struck is "loved by lightning."

So far as I have noticed, the particular species of tree most likely to be badly smashed or blown to pieces by lightning is the fir. I cannot account for this, unless it be due to a peculiar combination—much moisture, which is a good conductor for lightning, and much pitch and rosin, which are supposed to be almost nonconductors. At any rate, I have seen numbers of fir trees from forty to one hundred feet high that were cut down to the roots by a single stroke.

Over an extensive area on Mount Meeker, Colorado, balsam fir is the species which shows the most lightning wounds, with limber pine second in numbers. Yet the dominant species in this zone, which lies between the altitudes of nine thousand and eleven thousand feet, is the Engelmann spruce. The spruce is several times as numerous as the other two species combined, and in most areas is the taller. It is possible that it is struck with equal frequency but rarely receives wounds that record the experience. In the fir a slit or burst rent through the bark down one side of the tree was the lightning's mark. This is the common lightning sign.

I have always considered storms especially good exhibitions, and during camping trips often sought a commanding place to watch one. From the rim of a canyon, the top of a towering cliff, and windswept treetops I have watched rain, hurrying clouds, and illuminating lightning. These spectacular displays, with the rumbling roar aroused and repeated by the mountains, were among the most stirring contributions to my outings. Each experience was an adventure, and never was a storm in any way dull.

Sometimes lightning is a high explosive. One of the many

surfaces of which it gave me happened near my camp in Arizona. The bolt struck and wrecked the roots of the tree like a high explosive shell, blowing the trunk and top uninjured into the air. Lightning another time struck the side of a tree like a projectile and tore out a chunk of wood, then completely wrecked a tree several yards beyond. A lodgepole pine about sixty feet high, and without a limb for forty feet, was struck about twelve feet above the earth and cut off as though by a shell. Neither the stump below nor the trunk or top showed any trace of the bolt. Another time lightning struck the top of a tree and ran down the trunk into the earth where it apparently came in contact with the roots of another tree standing several yards off. Both trees were blown into the air, together with the rocks in which their roots were entangled.

Twice I have known bolts to wreck entire clumps of trees. One of these contained nine and the other five trees. Another bolt near my camp in southern Colorado blew all the leaves off a cottonwood clump without other visible injury.

Neither the wood in lightning-struck trees nor the chunks of exploded ones as a rule shows signs of heat or fire injury. Limbs of a lightning-struck oak in southern Colorado, however, were shattered and frayed out so that they appeared more like shredded hemp than anything else.

On examining a tree that I saw struck, there were two parallel lines of rupture grooves about four inches apart down the trunk. Either the bolt had divided before striking the tree, or else two bolts had struck the tree at about the same spot and instant.

Apparently a bolt striking a treetop follows down the grain of the wood—follows even the intensive twists of a tree from the top, where it strikes, to the earth. In some trees this twist of the grain was so spiral that the bolt passed three times around the tree trunk in its descent to the earth.

Usually the bolt plows a tiny U-shaped groove through the bark without otherwise injuring the tree. The lightning-struck tree, unless shattered to pieces, usually survives, but the openings which the lightning makes through the bark allow the entrance of insect enemies which frequently are detrimental.

There is not a complete agreement as to just what produces

Travelers at the edge of the clouds.

this wrecking explosiveness of lightning strokes. It is generally believed that the explosion is due to the superheated steam in the tree trunk. In most cases the injuries are slight and the tree lives on.

I doubt if more than one percent of the lightning-struck trees are set on fire. Of course it is the dead tree that is most inflammable, but many times lightning fires the trash accumulated against the base of a green tree. Lightning struck a green spruce on a slope visible from my camp. In a few minutes a column of smoke enveloped the tree. Then rain poured down. Half an hour later I found that a square yard of trash and spruce needles at the foot of the tree had been fired before the rain drowned the fire.

One evening in the Mesa Verde National Park lightning struck a dead pine on a canyon rim opposite where I was camping. There was no sign of fire at the time. A steady rainfall continued for three or four hours after the stroke, but about midnight the tree-top burned off and fell with a crash. I leaped up to see sparks and chunks of fire bounding down the side of the canyon, while the tall snag held up a flaming torch. May it not be that lightning, by starting a woods fire, brought Fire to our primitive ancestors, if not to all tribes, at least to many of them?

The ancients are said to have had many excellent legends concerning lightning. One of the most appealing and poetic that I have heard says that originally all the river channels of the earth were plowed by lightning.

Lightning is a common accompaniment of summer rains, and repeated lightning strokes may be the chief feature of a summer storm. Then again there may be a rain without lightning or thunder being seen or heard. Lightning is occasionally noticed during early spring and late autumn, and on rare occasions it makes startling appearances during winter storms.

Lightning seems to strike more frequently in the plains and valleys than in the mountains. During three hundred and five climbs to the top of Long's Peak I knew of lightning striking the summit but twice. Both bolts struck in precisely the same spot, and in both cases the storm clouds were high above the summit.

Most rain storms in high mountains are on the slopes, while

the peaks and high plateaus tower above in the sunshine. Sometimes the summit points are in the midst of the storm, but being in and not beneath the storm, they are therefore less frequently struck than the slopes or the lowlands. There may be exceptions in peaks of moderate height or those highly mineralized. When storms cover the mountains, the summits of peaks rarely are below—in range of—thunder bolts.

Peaks in the upper edge of the storm cloud are frequently enveloped in what may be called an invisible zone of electricity. This may ziz, ziz and crackle around rock points and give a tingle to the hair and finger tips, but there is no striking in this zone. Here the fluid may concentrate and descend upon lesser heights.

Though these so-called electrical storms are common on mountain peaks, I have not heard of their being fatal or even serious. As Muir says, they often cause every hair on one's head to stand up like an enthusiastic congregation and sing.

Lightning, however, is said to assail frequently the summit of Little Mount Ararat, Asia, and numbers of rocks on the top are shattered, bored through, and in places fused to glass by lightning strokes.

Lightning sometimes strikes a gravelly or sandy place and may penetrate for twenty feet or more, leaving a tiny, ragged-edged hole an inch or less in diameter. Around the edge of this the sand and stone are fused into glass or near glass. Sometimes a bolt penetrates solid rock and makes a glassy hole; but more often when rock is struck the bolt seems to explode as though resisted.

It was Benjamin Franklin who first thought to turn electrical energy into constructive work. And also it was he who brought forward the lightning-rod plan as a means of protecting buildings from lightning damage.

In May, 1904, I happened to be on Specimen Mountain, about 13,000 feet above the sea, during the gathering and the continuance of a storm which deluged and greatly damaged the lowlands of northern Colorado. There were frequent lightning strokes. The air was surcharged with juice. This twitched and contracted my muscles and pulled my hair with an accompaniment of snapping, crackling, buzzing, and humming.

The following day, while the storm was at its wildest in the lowlands, I was descending the mountains between eleven and nine thousand feet. Much of the time I was in the broken storm cloud, and, as I wrote in my notebook, "For two hours a crash and role of thunder was incessant. I counted twenty-three times that the lightning struck rocks, but I did not see it strike a tree."

Those who have not been in a violent thunder storm in rugged, high mountains perhaps cannot appreciate the remark of an old mountain guide who said, "The best thunders are always saved for the mountains." The mountain walls, cliffs, and long, receding slopes break, repeat, prolong, and compound the thunders into a deep-toned orchestra.

I have heard of people having their shoes burst off by a lightning bolt without their receiving serious injury. In Cripple Creek I saw a man at a windlass in an open space slightly injured by a lightning bolt which burst shoe-soles and uppers completely apart and tore off most of his clothing.

A dry, dead tree or limb is an extremely poor conductor. But during a rain when covered with a film of water these are converted into excellent conductors.

In the snowslide region of Mount Wetterhorn, Colorado.

Apparently a lightning bolt will not leave a good conductor for a poor one. While working in a tunnel extending nearly a thousand feet into a mountainside, lightning struck the water pipe outside and followed this into the tunnel, giving me a shake-up. All the way through the tunnel the pipe was in contact with the dry rocks. But my foot resting on the pipe was covered with a water-soaked shoe.

The records of the Agricultural Department indicate that lightning strikes far more frequently through the east than through the west, Illinois and Florida being most frequently struck. Yet in these states death and damage from lightning are almost negligible.

It is extremely rare for a big wild animal to be struck by lightning. Yet the woods and the mountains are peopled with moose, deer, elk, bear, and mountain sheep. Birds and squirrels, however, with roosts and nests in the treetops and woodpeckers with homes in tree trunks, are occasionally killed.

Once I was out for a few days with a burro, Satan, who was totally depraved. He wanted to leave undone everything that he was asked to do. In all his dreams a self-starter had not occurred to him. Once in motion he had but one speed—always on low. I found myself wondering if lightning had any affinity for burros. Satan was supposed to be the burden bearer of the expedition. Yet under a psychological test or in the field test his usefulness should have been rated low and I personally told him that he was wholly nonessential to this so-called vacation trip and to the happiness of the world as well. A vigorous expenditure of energy and expletive did not get us anywhere.

One day we turned into camp during a downpour of rain. We asked Satan to move a few yards farther that we might unpack under the shelter of a tree. With feet outbraced at every corner, two storms failed to move him. He pretended to go to sleep while we removed our bedding in the rain.

Just as the last of the pack was removed, two terrific lightning bolts struck close by. These resounding crashes instantly put life and fear into Satan. When a smashed treetop fell near him he rose on his hind legs and put his arms affectionately around me, hitting me over the eye with one shod hoof. I tolerated this demonstration simply because except for his firmness we would have been in the shelter of the tree which the lightning had hit on the head.

Once I watched two black and broken cloud strata that were piled against the horizon with a misty peak of summit cloud a thousand feet or more up in the sky. From this cloud peak there burst out together three golden rivers of lightning. These separated, ran vertically down the sky several thousand feet, and united in the lower cloud stratum. A number of times in the mountains I had seen shafts, zig-zag flashes, and sinuous golden lightning burst out of an absolutely clear, blue sky and descend to the earth. I have also seen trees struck by what appeared to be a golden ball of lightning which rolled into the tree horizontally. On one occasion a globe was followed by a number of other golden globes which traveled slowly over the same course.

Once near camp I saw both golden globes and golden rivers of lightning playing liquid fire over high mountains against the clear stars of night. These spectacular fireworks were accompanied with rumbling and crashing as though a violent thunder storm was in progress, yet nowhere in the sky or on the horizon was there a cloud in sight. The only possible explanation I could make of this exhibition was that beyond and below the high mountain horizon, and not many miles off, a storm was in progress.

The best thing in life is sentiment, and the best sentiment is that which is born of accurate knowledge.

Nature Study is seeing what one looks at and drawing proper conclusions from what one sees.

Happiness is nothing more or less than pleasant and efficient thinking.

The person who actually knows the pussy willow will know how to become acquainted with the potato bug. He will introduce himself.

—Liberty Hyde Bailey.

Landmarks

Landmarks and their surrounding scenes form pictures which every frontiersman or outdoor person learns to keep in mind. The explorer and the scout frequently look back, also to the right and to the left. Sometime the trail may be retraced, the landmark may be seen from the opposite direction, or the trail may be crossed. For the outdoor person to know where he is, to know what lake, cliff, meadow, or spring is to the north, south, east, and west of him is the most important part of all woodcraft.

This information prevents one becoming lost. It enables the prospector to return to the place where the rock outcrop carrying gold was discovered. It is both interesting and necessary for one who enjoys the outdoors to be able to return to the lightning-struck tree, the almost hidden beaver colony, the nest of the hummingbird, and to recall the peculiarities of a particular place and its distance from the orchid or the bear sign which he saw. Like a poet he must be able to give to each special thing a local habitation and individual character.

Looking back along the blazed trail of memory are numerous adventures and incidents that remain a part of my mental possessions and stand out as landmarks in my life.

I had done much camping without experiencing any serious difficulty in starting my campfire, even during the worst of weather. But one winter, when I was exploring the Medicine Bow Mountains—alone, as usual—I had a fire-building adventure which makes me shudder when I recall it.

On my way across a high pass I was caught on a steep, smooth, icy slope in a high wind. It was too cold to stop, and descent had to be made with utmost caution and freezing slowness. Though the wall-like, sixty-degree slope was constantly hugged closely, the wind a number of times saw how nearly possible it was to wipe me off without doing so. The mercury in my pocket thermometer barely showed above the zero mark, and all warming perfor-mances—hurrying, arm swinging, and dancing—were impossible on the icy, windswept steep.

I was chilled and benumbed almost beyond movement when the slope commenced to flatten out among the dwarfed and hardy spruces on the uppermost limits of tree growth. A quarter of a mile down in the woods was a doorless and deserted cabin in which I hoped to spend the night, but with stiffened muscles almost paralyzed with cold it required long and persistent effort to reach the place.

So chilled was I, that my benumbed condition did not shake off even after much kicking and arm-swinging in the cabin. Some of my muscles when moved had a feeling akin to that of "my foot is asleep."

After special attention to my right hand, it revived sufficiently to clasp the hatchet handle, but half an hour must have elapsed after my arrival at the cabin before a few small chunks were hacked from a fallen tree. With these and pitch splinters from my pocket I attempted to start a fire in the old fireplace of the cabin.

One end of each pitch splinter was hammered into a brush-like condition. My benumbed fingers would not hold a match. A number of matches were poured on the floor and a frosted thumb and finger tried in vain to clutch one. Lying on the floor and trying with both hands also was a failure. In desperation I tried to pick up a match between my chattering teeth. After mashing my cold, stiffened lips, I got the match into position at one side of my mouth. The match was lighted by scratching it across a stone with a turn of my head. With lips scorching, I rolled over and brought the blazing match in contact with the pitch splinters. These instantly and eagerly blazed up.

I made special efforts, after this nip-and-tuck experience, to learn the best ways of fire starting when both weather and fuel conditions were unfavorable, or when wit and muscle were dull or clumsy from cold or exhaustion. During long winter snowshoe trips it was my custom to have three separate stocks of matches: a leather box, a metal box, and a package of matches wrapped in oiled, waterproof silk which was sewed into my shirt pocket. The metal box was usually carried in a trousers pocket, and the leather one, which would resist water for hours, in a coat pocket. Generally the matches were the black-tipped sulphur ones.

Men have become so chilled and helpless that they have perished after reaching shelter because unable to hold a match with which to start a fire.

If the fingers are too cold to clutch and strike a match, this may be accomplished by catching the match up in the hand along with a stick an inch or less in diameter, or with the hatchet handle. The match may also be held and struck by binding it to a stick, as though to a splint, with a turn of a handkerchief, or with two or three turns of bark, or a string. Or it may be bound to a finger or a thumb. With fingers of both hands helpless the match may be held by getting it between two flat sticks which may be held between both hands.

Starting a fire in a pinch is what wins.

Fate was kind enough to cast me early in life where I formed the acquaintance of the wild folk. Bears, beavers, birds, chipmunks, and coyotes came strangely into my youthful life.

From the time I realized that animals and birds play merrily and frequently, wild life and wild places appealed to me with intensified interest. My estimate of wild folks rose mightily and the watching of wild life at play has claimed a large share of my outings and has given me an interest that never grows old.

The otter builds a slide on which to play; the whale often plays; the solemn grizzly bear plays merrily alone. Birds dance and play. Play appears to be a common and enlivening and beneficial habit in the entire world of wild life.

Chipmunks were the easiest animals to tame. Usually inside of an hour after one appeared I was able to get near him and often to feed him from my fingers.

Copeland Lake, Mount Copeland in the background.

A number of friendly chipmunks were taking peanuts from my hand as I sat one day in the doorway of my cabin. Occasionally one climbed upon my head. Suddenly around the corner of the cabin came another chipmunk pursued by a weasel. The weasel stopped with a show of anger at my presence. The frightened chipmunk fell exhausted in front of us.

When this stranger commenced to revive he showed astonishment at the intimacy of the other chipmunks and myself. Evidently his parents had taught him that there was no "safety first" for chipmunks but to flee from man and weasels. He looked at me nervously for a few seconds. I talked to him but he still appeared frightened. Then I took a step toward him. He turned to run, but evidently remembered the weasel, and stood up to look and listen. As there were no signs of his pursuer he turned for another look at the chipmunks and me.

At this instant a friendly beggar raced up and took a peanut from my fingers. The stranger could not believe his eyes; he rose on tip-toe to watch us. He came slowly six steps toward us, then at once retreated four. As nothing happened he presently joined the playing chipmunks. One scolded and another literally kicked him over, but he hung near. I threw him a peanut. He grabbed it, scampered to a nearby log and, standing erect, ate it. Then he came close for another. The following day he took a nut from my hand.

The chipmunks spent seven months of each year underground. The other five months they hustled about digging new tunnels for winter quarters, gathering winter food, sometimes scolding the magpies, and once in a while playing with the rabbits. They spent hours at a time making these tunnel homes, piling the earth out on the grass. Ofttimes they left their work and came hurrying to see me with their faces very dirty; a chunk of dry earth frequently stood up on the end of the chipmunk's nose. They enjoyed a dust bath. Now and then a chipmunk dusted himself so thoroughly that he appeared more like a gray ground squirrel than a chipmunk with black and brown stripes.

While still a boy I built a log cabin in the Rocky Mountains of Colorado and made my home there. For a number of years there was only one other cabin within miles. Few people came to see me; birds and animals were my callers, visitors, and neighbors. The region was ideal for a wide range of wild life. There were scattered pines and aspen around my cabin which stood in an open valley. On the mountain slope above grew a dense spruce forest. Below, a lively brook rushed through a willow-dotted meadow. I often saw deer that came to the brook to drink, and I spent many hours watching the activities of the beavers that established a colony on the stream.

Nearly all the birds and smaller animals were friendly toward me from the start; they were just as eager to know me as I was to know them. I was interested in every living thing. I welcomed the wild people large and small and all quickly learned that I was not dangerous and that nothing around my cabin was ever killed. In a little while bluebirds, wrens, chickadees, camp-birds, crested jays, robins, rabbits, squirrels, and chipmunks not only trusted me but ofttimes rushed to me for safety when frightened and when threatened by their enemies. They showed their interest in this place of safety, and my cabin became the center of a little wild life reservation.

Two bluebirds built beneath the end of the ridgepole over the door before the cabin was completed. They were confiding from the start, but not until the first eggs were hatched did they take time to call upon me. One afternoon Mrs. Blue flew in and circled the room and as she went out her mate came in. The next time both came in together and curiously examined a number of objects on the table. After this they often alighted upon my shoulders and ate from my hands.

A wren often sang outside while I stood within reach and sometimes, too, came into the cabin for something to eat, but he never alighted upon me nor ate from my fingers.

Except in summer, flocks of chickadees came every few days. The first flock that I welcomed looked at me and called sweetly to one another. I stood close and talked to them, offering something to eat, but they went on busily feeding from limb to limb. They were sometimes scattered over and through two nearby trees at once. One day a flock stopped for a merry visit. Two, three, four, the entire flock, alighted on me, all merrily calling "chick-a-de-de-dee." Momentarily chickadees took possession of me—head, arms, and shoulders. Then they flew forward, one or more at a time, constantly calling to one another so that none would be left behind. These cheerful little people always seemed happy in their food-hunting rambles.

Within a minute after the first camp-birds called they were eating from my hand. They are a confiding bird wherever found. While they were with me they were most gentle, chatting in low tones and moving about deliberately. They never remained more than a few minutes. They live among dense evergreen forests and do not seem to like the open, but they made me occasional visits the year round.

The haughtiest, lordliest, and wisest bird visitor was the long-crested jay, with dark blue coat and with top of head and crest jet-black. They were ever reserved, and though trusting me, never became confiding. They came every day during the winter months, but in summer went away to Canada and Alaska.

Every living thing responded in its own way. Sometimes a bird came close and by looks and actions appeared to be trying to speak. It required a long time and even special efforts with a few species of birds and animals before they understood that it was safe to be near me. Once they lost fear they became curiously, watchfully interested in every move I made.

The shy, nervous rabbits at last made up their minds that I was not ferocious. Then they would come to feed in the yard during the daytime. I discovered they were out more often during cloudy days than during sunny ones. On a bright day they always sat or fed around the edge of a tree shadow, never putting a nose or an ear out in the sunshine, unless hopping to another place of safety. Evidently shadows were camouflage against hawks or other enemies; in shadow was "safety first." The rabbits were with me the year round.

While my pony was eating rock salt in the meadow one autumn day a wild mountain sheep—a Bighorn—came up and joined her. The sheep saw me approaching and ran off while I was still a quarter of a mile away. The few days later he came again for salt. I had moved the block of salt nearer the cabin. The sheep circled it a few times and retreated, but came back that afternoon. The next time he came I stood within a stone's throw of the salt. He came almost to it, then turned and ran away at high speed. A month later he returned and found the salt in the same place. I stood within a stone's throw. Carrying himself erect and alert, he advanced with frequent stops to the salt and licked it for a minute or longer. The following summer he finally came to the salt when I sat near it.

Thus on the installment plan we became acquainted, or rather, salt and safety brought us together. One afternoon he stood boldly looking me over at a distance of thirty feet. I embarrassed him by asking: "How is the weather on the heights?" He jerked his head up-and-down. I asked: "Which crag did you last climb?" Then he lost his fear and was curious. One day, after seven years of friendly advances, he came boldly to my cabin and he licked salt from my hand.

The home of the Bighorn is among the mountain tops. This one lived on a plateau that was 12,000 feet above sea level. Here he spent the winter as well as the summer, but now and then he made an excursion into the lowlands. I noticed that he came down for the earliest green grass near my cabin, which was at least three weeks earlier in appearing than the green grass on the plateau up in the sky. Sometimes he came for salt. Generally he came down for some definite thing, but now and then the sheep left the heights with no particular purpose.

Occasionally I saw where a bear had been ambling along the brook, and more often I saw where one had been in a ravine only a minute's walk from my cabin. Bears are big, shy people, but they quickly learn of places where they are welcome. They are not savage or ferocious, but harmless, full-of-fun fellows, unless shot at or chased with dogs, and prefer playing to fighting. Early mornings I often went out hoping to find one. One morning, while climbing a mountainside near my cabin, I heard the breaking and tearing of rotten logs behind a tree clump, and slipped around to get a glimpse of whatever it was through the spruce woods.

It was a big, brown grizzly bear. Just the tips of his fur were silvery. He was seated dog-like by a large, half-rotten stump, eating ants and grubs. Every few seconds he reached out with right fore paw and ripped loose a chunk of the stump, and then licked it with his tongue. Three or four times he dug into the torn stump with his right paw and picked up something which he put in his mouth. He was an interesting sight, somewhat like a great puppy. His eating with one paw and being right-handed most impressed me.

In the midst of his eating he scented me, stood on his hind legs, looked calmly in my direction for three or four seconds, and then lumbered off through the woods, stopping only once to look back. After a short while I followed his trail. Where he had crossed a brook he left a track in the mud that looked very much like the track of a barefooted man.

One day I saw him in a wild raspberry patch, biting off the tops of the vines, and eating vines, thorns, leaves, and berries. That afternoon I saw him catching mice in the edge of a grassy place close to a beaver pond. Most bears live upon berries, roots, grass, grasshoppers, mice, and other small animals. Consuming so many pests and dead animals, their food habits make them useful to man. Rarely does a bear kill a big animal, wild or tame. *They never eat human flesh.*

I raised two lively grizzlies. These were caught in the nearby woods when tiny cubs, each about the size of a rabbit. They were playful and friendly; they had merry times boxing, wrestling, digging, and tumbling about in the water. Johnny and Jenny were never cross and were the most wide-awake youngsters that I have ever seen.

Bears always interested me. The grizzly is considered the greatest wild animal in the world. He has strength, speed, endurance, and impressive size. He attends to his own affairs. He is curious concerning everything strange that he sees, readily adjusts himself to new conditions, and is never stupid. Bears are threatened with extermination and need protection.

The wilderness is one of the safest and the most interesting places on earth. Early in my life I had a camping trip with the great John Muir in the mountains of California. He told me that he had tramped the mountains of the West alone and without a gun and

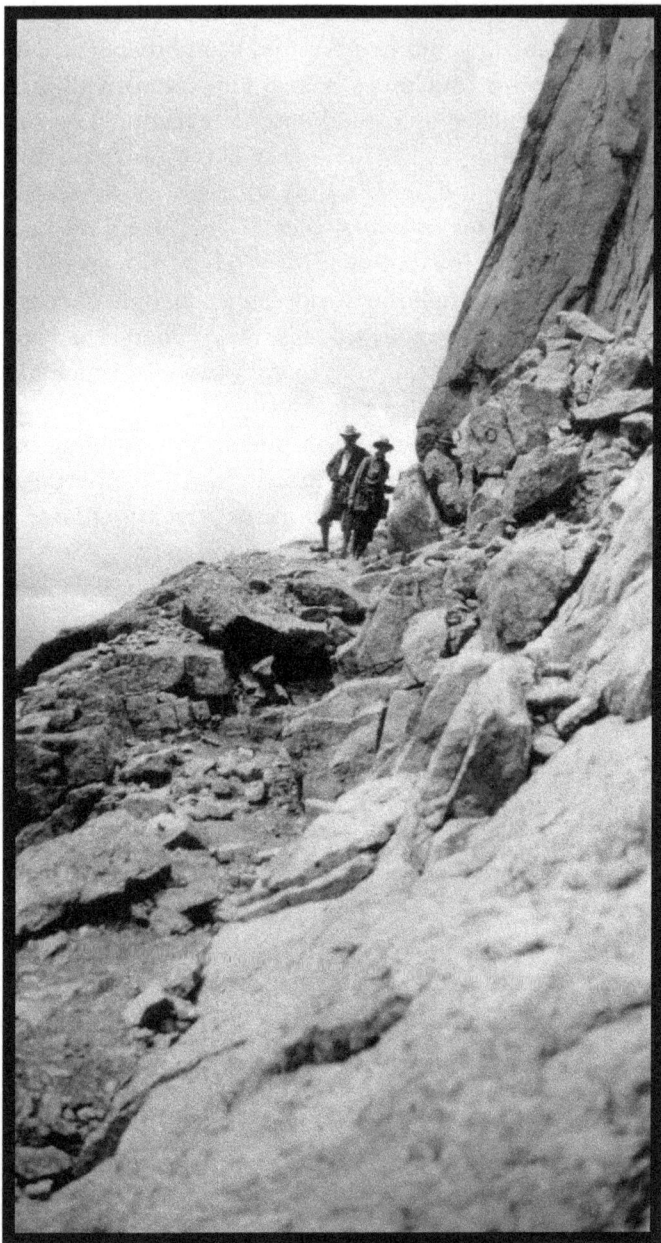

Climbers on Long's Peak.

nothing had ever attacked him. Such has been my experience.

The camera adds purpose and interest to an outing. It is educational and develops the artistic and the habit of seeing the beautiful—of looking for the best. A cloud-piercing peak, wild mountain sheep, beaver colonies, a waterfall touched with light and shadow, and many other pictures are ever in waiting. These will preserve with startling, delightful fidelity the interesting experiences of the trip.

Recently the region in which I enjoyed wilderness folk when a boy became a wild life reservation through the making of the Rocky Mountain National Park. With the increased numbers of wild life reservations and national parks in which animals are never shot at, the boys and girls of the country will have an opportunity to become better acquainted with all the wild animals, large and small; to watch easily bears and beavers, birds and butterflies.

These national parks are also wild flower reservations. In them the geological wonders, the forests, the wild bloom, the folk in fur and feathers are protected for their higher values, for uses in education, for employment, for giving relaxation and universal sympathy, for inspiring vision, and for enriching the imagination.

These wilderness places are Happy Hunting Grounds for all and in them the nature guide has supreme opportunities for useful and ennobling service.

Every child should have mud pies, grasshoppers, water bugs, tadpoles, frogs, mud-turtles, elderberries, wild strawberries, acorns, chestnuts, trees to climb, brooks to wade in, water-lilies, woodchucks, bats, bees, butterflies, various animals to pet, hayfields, pine cones, rocks to roll, sand, snakes, huckle-berries, and hornets; and any child who has been deprived of these has been deprived of the best part of his education.

—Luther Burbank.

We read and studied out of doors, preferring the sunlit woods to the house. All my early lessons have in them the breath of the woods—the fine, resinous odour of pine needles blended with the perfume of wild grapes. Seated in the gracious shade of a wild tulip tree, I learned to think that everything has a lesson and a suggestion...Indeed, everything that could hum, or buzz, or sing, or bloom, had a part in my education—noisy-throated frogs; katydids and crickets held in my hand until, forgetting their embarrassment, they trilled their reedy note, little downy chickens and wild flowers; the dogwood blossoms; meadow-violets and budding fruit trees. I felt the bursting cotton-bolls and fingered their soft fiber and fuzzy seeds; I felt the low soughing of the wind through the cornstalks; the silky rustling of the long leaves; and the indignant snort of my pony, as we caught him in the pasture and put the bit in his mouth—ah me! how well I remember the spicy, clovery smell of his breath!

—Helen Keller.

Children of My Trail School

One summer day nearly twenty years ago a number of boys and girls appeared at my Rocky Mountain cabin. They wanted me to go with them to the old beaver colony. A boy and a girl started making the request, but before they could finish every child was asking me to go. "It is more than two miles," I told them, "and we must walk." This but added to their desire to go at once.

Stepping softly and without saying a word, we slipped through the woods and peeped from behind the last trees into a grassy opening by the beaver pond, hoping for a glimpse of a coyote or a deer. Then we examined the stumps of aspens recently cut by the beavers. We walked across the dam. We made a little raft of logs and went out to the island house in the pond. Then we built tiny beaver houses and also dugouts in the bank. We played we were beavers.

On the way home we turned aside from the trail to investigate a delightful bit of forested wilderness between two brooks. We were explorers in a new country. The grove was dense and full of underbrush. It was voted to send out a likely boy and girl to discover how many hundred miles it was through the forest. While waiting we decided to examine one of the brooks, which someone called the Amazon River. We found a delta which one boy insisted was the delta at the mouth of the Mississippi. No one objected and we had discussions concerning deltas, large and small. The vast wilderness between our two brooks—which contained really about one acre—was reported by our two scouts as altogether too large for us ever to explore.

Someone then proposed we should cross the brook on a fallen log to see who the strange people were in the wilderness on the other side. The last boy of the party made a long jump from the end of the log and declared he had jumped across a nation—that one boundary line was the end of the log and the other was where he alighted. Just where the remaining two lines should be provoked a profound discussion, as boundary lines of nations often do. It was finally agreed that the other lines should be determined by one of the girls taking a hop, skip, and jump.

We decided to take a census and at once everyone began to count the inhabitants of this nation. We found a number of bugs, spiders, and beetles; then other beetles and a few grasshoppers; and finally everyone surrounded a swarming ant hill, trying to determine how to make an accurate count of this warlike and numerous tribe. This was never settled, for suddenly a big grasshopper with black and yellow wings entered the nation from the outside. He alighted for only a moment and then flew away again. The opinion was about equally divided as to whether he should be counted as one of the inhabitants or an invader.

At this stage someone broke the news that it was already too late for us to reach home for lunch. So intense had been the interest that we had forgotten even to keep track of mealtime.

Two likely boys were sent out to forage for rations, with suggestions that they go to the kitchen and procure supplies enough to prevent starvation among the explorers until night, and return by the shortest route.

While we were eating merrily round a campfire by the brook a wasp and a fly engaged in a struggle on a mountainside. The top of the mountain was no higher than the knee of the boy who stood by it. When this life and death struggle ended by the contestant falling over a precipice thousands of feet below, everyone concluded it was time to go home.

That evening these excited and enthusiastic boys and girls related the day's experience to anyone who would listen. They had been explorers in a wilderness, had camped by mighty rivers, had seen wild animals and strange nations. Their imaginations were on fire. This world has become an inexhaustible wonderland.

These children were dealing with real things through interest, and their imaginations blazed with more keenness than it was possible for the powers of legends and fairy tales to incite. They had been to school, had studied, had worked, had learned without realizing it. Their reports amounted to enthusiastic recitations of new, big lessons well learned. Best of all, they were happy, and were eager to go on with this schooling—this developing. We have continued these excursions somewhat irregularly through the years to the present time and handled them with increasing effectiveness.

While a guide on Long's Peak I developed what may be called the poetic interpretation of the facts of nature. Scientific names in a dead language together with classifications that dulled interest were ever received, as they should have been, with indifference and lack of enthusiasm by those who did not know. Hence I began to state information about most things in the form of its manners and customs, its neighbors and its biography.

Nature's storybook is everywhere and always open. And I wish children might have everywhere what the children have had here in enjoyment, educational foundation, and incentive. What we are doing here may be done elsewhere.

John Muir, in writing his boyhood experiences, says: "The

animals about us were a never-ending source of wonder and delight. How utterly happy it made us! Nature streaming into us, wooingly teaching her wonderful, glowing lessons so unlike the dismal, grim ashes and cinders so long thrashed into us. Here, without knowing it, we still were in school; every wild lesson a love lesson, not whipped but charmed into us."

Interest gives the ability and energy to see accurately and the incentive to watch for things that may happen around us; adds purpose to every outdoor day. Such happy experiences based on interest truly enrich life. Agassiz said that his chief claim to distinction was that he had taught men to observe. Interest is the master teacher.

The Robinson Crusoe School was the name someone early applied to us, but later the name Trail School was taken. This school—the great outdoors—is in session whenever children wander over the trail, free from academic chaperonage. The trail supplies materials and equipment, and Mother Nature is an endless mental stimulus.

We are in a high mountain valley, in one corner of the Rocky Mountain National Park, at an altitude of nine thousand feet. The locality is rich in natural history. Within three miles of us there are hundreds of varieties of flowers; dozens of kinds of birds; a number of wild animals, including beavers and bears; forests of pine, fir, spruce, and aspen; steep mountains; likely streams, and a number of kinds of rocks.

The Trail School is little more than a name, plus results. There is no organization, no staff; no opening, no closing. It has no courses of study, no set times for study, no set tasks, no grade cards. The children follow any interest that appeals, and when it appeals. They are never asked to pursue anything distasteful, in fact, any given subject or for any given period. There are no recitations and no examinations. Competition, as ordinarily known, does not exist. There are no prizes for excellence, no honors for advancement.

Each child is too busy acquiring additional facts to concern himself about having more or less than his companions. He is not studying for a preparatory school or for college. We strive to see to it that these children continually use their faculties, honoring facts rather than authority. Books we highly prize, but their place is made wholly secondary and incidental.

Information given the children is tied up with life, connected with neighbors, and given a place or a part in things going on. The following will show our usual way of answering a question:

Walking along the summit of a rocky ridge, we rounded a cliff and came upon an aged and picturesque tree. One child asked what all wanted to know, the name—what kind of tree it was. We speculated concerning the life of this old tree; wondered concerning storms that had struck it. We noticed that its arms were long—so long that the tree was wider than high; we measured its height and its diameter; noted the color and character of its bark. A last year's cone on the ground looked as though varnished; the unripe ones on the tree were grass-green. Then we examined the needles; they were fastened on the branches in little bundles of five. At last we concluded that it must be a limber pine.

"I remember reading about it in John Muir's 'The Mountains of California,'" said one child. "He often found it growing on dry, rocky, windswept ridges."

When a new boy or girl arrives he or she is generally full of movie talk or train experience, or eager to find out concerning riding, fishing, or other long-treasured plans. But these outing children talk. Presto! Change! The new arrival edges toward mother and begs to join the young explorers next day.

We ask the children not to discuss either personalities or the movies. One evening a number of boys were about to leave with sleeping bags to camp for the night in a beaver colony, when a new boy, fresh from the city and the movies, came along. He joined them. He talked incessantly concerning the movies. As soon as sleeping bags were piled and before wood was gathered for a campfire two of the boys led the movie one off behind a clump of fir trees and demanded from him whether he would stop movie talk or if he would make it necessary for them to beat him up. It squelched him. Nevertheless, during this trip he picked up a new interest.

We have yet to find a lazy child. Minds and muscles move

willingly. Again and again we have been assured that this or that child could not or would not learn. But under Trail School environment he formed new habits. Under the zest and spell of interest he joyfully and tellingly applied himself. These children are one hundred percent concentrated. They have the burning morale of interested youth. They are doing things. They want to do still other things. They want to learn. Many of their activities would be classed as work—except by themselves.

To help complete a flower exhibition two girls and two boys voluntarily climbed nearly twenty-five hundred feet up the mountainside. When they had gathered the desired plants they made a side trip for another rare flower. Two of these children were considered dull and lazy; yet how energetic and concentrated they were—an excellent illustration of how interest and development create and administer discipline!

The mountain trail is a part of the earth's most influential environment. It is an avenue of interest. It mingles life, motive, opportunity, and desire. Whoever travels the trail is enjoying living and learning; is going somewhere. In trail environment Mother Nature mingles facts and fun, and the traveler readjusts himself to its conditions and develops along the way.

With a party of more than twenty we one day cooked our lunch over a campfire. We used little sticks for the fire and kept it as small as possible. As Indians were supposed to be after us we burned every scrap of refuse and carefully covered the ashes with a flat rock. Being clean is the most concealing camouflage for a camp. When we left it the place did not look as though anyone had ever camped there. Although we had twenty in this party we generally limited the number to five or six.

Trailing appears to be the supreme outdoor experience. Sometimes we follow the track of a deer or a horse; at other times one of the party travels for ten minutes from a given point and is allowed to conceal his trail in every way he can think of. At the word we set off eagerly to follow this concealed trail. There is concentration, enthusiasm, and application. In following a trail of any kind the girls frequently excel the boys.

One of our excursions was an exciting two-day search for the source of a stream. We found it above the limits of tree growth in a little pool at the foot of a cliff. There were mountain sheep tracks by it. On the tiny stream each boy and girl launched a boat—the tiny leaf of an alpine plant—which was to report promptly, with its message, to some boy or girl in New Orleans.

We tried out our noses. Polemonium, with blossoms of peculiar and pungent odor, is called skunkweed. The children were blindfolded and asked to find an interesting flower, blooming about twenty-five feet from them, which was sending wireless signals for the nose. Merry times they had seeking for it. In all succeeding trips that we made there was increased and enjoyable use of the sense of smell.

We tasted and smelled the bark and needles of the balsam fir tree as an important preliminary to searching for it that night with our noses. Anyone who desired was allowed to supplement taste and touch also. A little girl who was the first to find it was not certain until she had touched the tree to which her nose led her.

One windy day we were exploring a dense primeval forest when the sound of a cascading brook reached our ears. We stopped to listen and to separate the flowing tones of the water from similar sounds the wind made in the pines. Then we tried to determine the direction to the brook, and also the distance, by the sounds of the water.

In a comparatively open level place we walked round and noted the boulders and the trees. One at a time was then blindfolded and asked to find a particular tree or boulder.

One of the incidents I sometimes tell to heighten the interest when we are training our senses is of several blind men in Wheeling, West Virginia, who walked more than a mile one winter night to hear me lecture. Another is of a blind Indian in British Columbia who took me several miles up and then down a swift mountain stream, guided by touch, sound, and his imagination.

Many a time the children and I drew maps and pictures with sticks in the sand. Sometimes we set down a part of the multiplication table. On a big sand map we located beaver colonies, big trees, little trees, places where we had camped, places where we had seen mountain sheep, places we had explored. One of the places the children best remembered was the top of the Twin Peaks, where we had lain down and with magnifying glasses carefully looked at the tiny dwarf flowers. Another was that strange timberline of dwarfed and twisted trees on the side of Long's Peak. Still another was Chasm Lake, an utterly wild place, where there were ice-piles, snow-drifts, flowers, and lichened rocks; and where a big, fat woodchuck had come out to eat scraps of lunch from our fingers. On the sand map we also marked places unexplored—spots where we hoped soon to go and to make discoveries.

We try to develop in the child mind the spirit of exploration, so he may enjoy the search for facts, both in books and in the outdoors. Before long he eagerly hunts through books or appeals to individuals to satisfy some interest roused on the trail. The results have been immeasurable and inspiring. With eye and ear and nose the children gather rare materials—materials that arouse reflection, imagination, reasoning; the brain is growing.

A nature library is kept convenient for the children and they use it with inspiring enthusiasm. In this library are the best works obtainable on natural history: books concerning birds, bears, beavers, insects, wild flowers, and forests, written by people with an intimate acquaintance with and an enthusiasm for their subjects. These are books filled with facts. There is not a single reference to fairies who rewarded good children; bears that ate bad children are not even mentioned. There are no billboards carrying morals in capital letters. There are no lessons either brutally blunt or with camouflage decorations. There are no textbooks.

Someone once called my attention to the fact that my nature library lacked the common books that were written about nature for children. These had not been intentionally omitted. I had never thought of them, nor, through the years, had a single child ever asked for one of them. So I believe for most practical purposes they may be classed as nonessentials.

One day while homeward bound, after two hours with the strange trees at timberline, we purposely came close to a large and nearly round boulder. All ran to examine it. We called it the Ice King's marble. Ice probably had taken it from the top of Long's Peak and carried it across a canyon. While the interest was on this boulder the whole glacial story was opened. From that hour these children had an eye for glacial topography and a mind for books concerning glaciers.

The children often wrote a delightful account of an experience or of their special interest. Such accounts were not booky, they were spontaneous. These compositions were what we desired but they were not required nor even lightly requested.

Generally in the study of zoology or botany the student begins with the far-away, primitive, and least interesting forms of life, and memorizes. We use the bird, animal, or flower at hand. We learned something of its life history, of its evolution; of its relation to surrounding plans and animals; of its enemies, its travels, its food; and sometimes how it has been changed by environment. We learn something of the year-round life of mountain sheep, of beavers and other animals, and of birds. Their popular names we use as a label or mark of identification; but we learn all we can before becoming serious concerning the name. In due time—and this is by the time scientific names and classifications mean something—the children find both interesting.

Our method has been efficient, whether the prescribed one or not. By it the boys and girls have laid the foundation for an education and learned many of the facts and principles of nature. And, what is important, they have learned that the outdoors is friendly.

Most people think that the wilderness is a supremely dangerous place for human beings. They carry through life a handicap of fear of the outdoors. These children learn that the wilds are not only friendly but hospitable; they find ferocious animals only in storybooks, and ere long being out after dark or in the rain is fun.

A well known educator recently emphasized the fact that to have a sane and healthful view of life it is necessary to have correct fundamental information concerning natural history; and that this knowledge can be acquired only by intimate contact with nature.

For two or three hours in a primeval forest we played that we were primitive people. The children had a glimpse of the child-hood of our race; learned something of the diet of primitive people; why we have so many domesticated plants. All this started over seeing mushrooms and wondering whether they were poisonous.

When out with nature the unexpected often happens. If we come upon something well worth while—like a mother bird leading her young from the nest, beavers at play, or a near view of mountain sheep—we remain and make the most of this opportunity.

Each new interest is opportunity. The interest is sometimes heightened by the children abruptly determining what is next to be seen. In the course of a month we use telescope, microscope, botanies, bird and animal books, and frequently call in the use of multiplication and percentage. The children have many irons in the fire. Only one is hot at a time; but how it is then hammered!

Anyone who goes with the children is considered by them a welcome outsider or a privileged guest, honored and consulted, but ever under their orders. However, that they should not come to depend on an older person accompanying them, I sometimes leave them as we start homeward. Sometimes they vote to return home under the orders of one of the children as leader. But several often go off together, or by twos, or even one alone.

Each child is encouraged to report anything of unusual interest. If a discovery is made—a crippled animal or a rare flower—he is to return at once and tell others about it. Sometimes scouts are sent out to look for young beavers, bear signs, or to see whether the first blue fringed gentians have bloomed.

There is a bulletin board in the nature room on which appear notices of future excursions, of discoveries, of special meetings, of exhibitions, of flowers, rocks, and other things wanted for these exhibitions, and recent outdoor photographs. When the children are not in the field a conference may be called at any time.

It was a stay-at-home day the morning a boy came rushing in to report that a side of a canyon had fallen in. Children hurried right and left to tell others, and in a few minutes all were off to see the landslide. They forgot to take lunch along. Eagerly they discussed the probable causes of this slide and also the results from it. It dammed the gulch and was already forming a pond. How long, we wondered, before water-loving plants and animals would come to live here.

This gave an excellent opportunity to discuss the supreme productive resource—soil. Other resources had their innings—water, forests, birds; and so, too, did erosion, topography, and streams. I had to tell of landslides I had seen and where the best accounts of big landslides might be read.

We were returning from a day's outing when we came upon an unextinguished campfire. "Here is a mighty forest fire!" I said. "How many will volunteer to fight it to a finish?" Instantly everyone volunteered. A boy was sent for help, a girl was sent for a pail of water. We fought and won. That night we read up on fire fighting.

We often walked home through the rain; during several downpours we deliberately went out into the storm. On a few gray days we climbed up the mountainside through a solid sky of clouds until we were above them in the sunshine. We also made little journeys after dark, visiting pine woods, beaver colonies, and streams; calling on hundreds of sleepy flowers; watching shadowy coyotes and owls and listening to their playful cries and calls.

The unfortunate attitude of the parent was an obstacle to every outing. Many were thrown almost into a panic when a trip for their children was proposed, and too often came out of the panic to condemn such excursions with all the vehemence of old error. Each new parent on the scene exhibited a misunderstanding of the outdoors.

We never had a serious accident, never were attacked by bears or any other wild animal, and never did a child even catch cold. These facts, together with the enthusiasm of the children for such outings and their obvious development, won out.

We discouraged the collecting of specimens, but we encouraged the bringing in of a mental record—an account of the day's experience. From now on we shall provide a book and encourage each child to write down the most important experience of the day as a part of the outing round. I should have done this long ago. I have lost many happy accounts.

A few unusual specimens collected by the children have been

preserved for their natural history association and their nature room. In this room they hold meetings. If a child comes upon something deemed rare, something that will be of general interest, he is encouraged to bring it in for the nature room. One afternoon the association unanimously decided to bring in a tree with an unusual history. All the children went along and its getting filled half a day for them full of thought and action.

This young pine, when twenty-one years of age, was knocked down by a fire-killed tree falling upon it. The top straightened up and made a loop almost around the dead tree that rested upon and distorted it. We learned the young pine's age from the annual growth rings in the stump, and also how many years it had lived before being injured and how many since.

Occasionally the children give an exhibition and invite the older people to see it. They plan these exhibitions and gather and arrange materials for them. While a rock exhibition was on we discussed geology, rock formations and transformations, vol-canoes, earthquakes, erosion, rock strata and color. During a flower exhibition we discussed the evolution of plants, pollination, interdependence with insects, and seed distribution.

Often I am too busy, or there are too many boys and girls, or it seems best to have someone else accompanying a party afield. But to find individuals who will do this without becoming teachy or preachy and deadly to the children is most difficult. Most teachers, some parents, and many others want us to ignore interest and desire and force of the children to memorize something which they consider worthwhile.

One day a well-known school superintendent offered to help us. He unfolded his plans in the presence of a number of the children. I wish you could have seen the effect of his words upon them! When he proposed classes and study, system and grading and examinations, each child heard the suggestions just as he would hear the threat of a probable whipping.

The academic mind—and in many respects the old puritanical mind—holds that things pleasurable and interesting are to be shunned; that they are akin to vice; that it is virtuous to do the disagreeable things, and all-important to force yourself to do what you do not like.

In human psychology it is ever important to get results while working under morale, using all the power that interest adds. Thus finally you accomplish the most difficult and greatest results through the supreme, sustained efforts that desire and interest make possible. Natural phenomena interest and stimulate the mind in a thousand ways.

We had a variety of kinds of excellent discipline. I sometimes think that discipline as it is applied in the school world actually dwarfs the senses and robs life of its interest. Mathematics, dead languages when not liked, drudgery, and disagreeable tasks usually dull those upon whom they are inflicted and develop half-hearted habits.

The psychology of youth calls for discipline of a different character. This is pleasurable discipline. These children frequently and cheerfully labor under severe, self-imposed discipline, and under this all their faculties are at their best. Fortunate is the child whose discipline is determined by its own inspiration. Interest makes play of the hardest work.

We sat for more than two hours upon a log by a beaver pond. When we had at last satisfied ourselves that muskrats—the little brothers of the beaver—were living in an abandoned beaver house, we started on and then questions and comments came thick and fast.

Sometimes we would count all the flowers that grew in a circle the diameter of which corresponded to the height of the shortest child in the party. Sometimes we counted all the trees in a given square.

Every normal child is as avaricious for information as a miser is for gold. This childish desire to know, to learn, will assure mental development if information be given in a way that appeals. Children can learn but little from cold, unrelated, segregated facts; from academic system and memorized rules. Hence, before the young are assigned to learn the definite cut-and-dried facts their elders deemed essential, they need the development that roused interest gives.

We try to use to the utmost the interest of the child. Interest a child and he thinks. While a child is thinking he is learning. One interest invariably leads to a larger and then to other interests.

Of an evening I listen willingly to their ideas and comments, and to their experiences. I endeavor to make comments that will cause the child to desire to go back and look again at the wonder things he has seen and at others which he apparently missed. I do all I can to stimulate his creative faculty. I ever try to answer his questions in a way that will add to his interest and, if possible, multiply or extend this interest.

If a child's lesser questions are answered he will presently come back with greater ones. Surely, the opportunity of one's life is to listen helpfully when the child is talking and to answer happily his eager questions!

The experiences these children have and their reflections concerning the things seen give them the ability to reason, and develop their observation and imagination. With these powers working, there is nothing that can obstruct a child's way to an education. He wants to learn and will find a way.

Sometimes in telling their experiences the children let themselves go and use their imagination freely. This is excellent. It is a healthy imagination; they simply expand, extend, or create the probable continuation of facts they have seen. There is nothing magical, nothing illogical, no monstrosity—just poetical interpretation of facts. When asked for the facts about what they have seen they give them accurately—the color, size, and the neighboring objects. They have really observed.

The average person does well to see with fifty percent efficiency. I have talked separately with three or four children concerning the same experience, and their accounts agreed; they must have run above ninety percent in accurate observation.

President Charles W. Eliot came out with the following sweeping statement in a recent publication by the United States Bureau of Education, called Certain Defects in American Education and the Remedies for them:

"It is the men who have learned—probably out of school—to see and hear correctly and to reason cautiously from facts observed, who carry on the great industries of the country and make possible great transportation systems and international commerce."

Doctor Elliott goes on to say:

"Since the United States went to war with Germany there has been an extraordinary exhibition of the incapacity of the American people, as a whole, to judge evidence, to determine facts, and even to discriminate between facts and fancies. This incapacity appears in the public press; in the prophecies of prominent administrative officials, both state and national; in the exhortations of the numerous commissions which are undertaking to guide American business and philanthropy; and in the almost universal acceptance by the people at large, day by day, of statements which have no foundation and of arguments in the premises of which are not facts or events, but only hopes and guesses.

"In most American schools there has been a lack of systematic training of the senses...to record, remember, and describe accurately observations made by his own senses. Little systematic training has been given day by day in the processes of determining facts and weighing evidence...Worst of all, most American schools have neglected to enlist and cultivate assiduously the interest of each pupil in his daily work, in spite of the obvious fact that no human being—child, adolescent, or adult—can do his best work unless he is taking an interest in that work.

"Remedies are the substitution of teaching by observation and experiment for much of the book work now almost exclusively relied on; the cultivation in the pupils of activity of body and mind during all school time—an activity which finds delight in the exercise of the senses and of the powers of expression in speech and writing; the insistence on the acquisition of personal skill of some sort; the stimulation in every pupil of interest in his work by making the object of it intelligible to him."

The Trail School methods appear to have developed the constant habit of accurate observation; of learning to see; looking with eager, interested eyes and seeing things as they are. Of an evening when the children are merrily recounting the experiences of the day we are impressed with the fact that they see accurately and recount truthfully, and judge by the evidence.

These children are in love with their activities. Burroughs had said that knowledge acquired without love will not stick. The most amazing things brought out by the Trail School are the accuracy with which the children see and acquire facts and correctness with which they describe what they had seen. It might be thought that our ways of doing things would make the children unsystematic; but when reached by that magnificent incentive called interest a child goes after anything—difficult, easy, pleasant, or otherwise. It is a joy to do it. We found that the children quickly developed the mental habit of being systematic just through interest. It was not long before a child systematically and persistently followed an interest by specializing upon it, thus forming the acquaintance also of the things related to it.

A few weeks of this meant one hundred percent health. The child learned to use his senses, learned to see and to hear; he accumulated facts, materials which compelled thought and developed the imagination. He became a reasoner. The mind grew like a wild garden. When it was all over most of the children had developed interests in world subjects that had not been even mentioned. They had sympathies—universal feelings. They were developing democratic actions and habits.

Above all, we try to develop the imagination, which has been called "the supreme intellectual faculty"—an imagination based on realities. This kind of imagination deals ever with cause and effect; it touches cold facts with fancy; gives the poetic interpretation—that is to say, with cause, effect, and vision, it shows possibilities of development.

A tree seed touched with imagination becomes a forest full of wilderness life in a natural manner, without enchantment or magic. A prospector dreams of gold and glory. He seeks it with a pick; never does he look for it at the foot of the rainbow, or expected as a reward from a king, or wait for a fairy to bring it.

Most legends and fairy stories mislead the mind and betray the imagination. Such magic ever dreams of castles in Spain. Mental mirages waste many a life.

The normal imagination hitches its wagon to a star or a mule, and the team travels merrily, whether it arrives or not. This imagination is based on realities; it is one that sees the logical and natural results or developments in advance and pictures glorious changes through natural growth or evolution, and never by magic or enchantment. This normal imagination is a combination of information and inspiration; it is creative, rouses effort, and gets results.

In brief, then, all we are trying to do may be stated as follows: We found that every child wanted to learn. He asked questions. He was interested. Our opportunity lay in the rightful answering of questions. These answers must appeal to the imagination. We tried in our answer to continue and multiply this interest by showing him something new, and more than he was expecting.

Often our answer was part of a story. We answered with words, stories, demonstrations, excursions, and even books. He was led into larger interests. Nature interested him most. Nothing discouraged him so long as he was interested. Interest may play out of work. We have never found a lazy child.

These answers gave impressions; gave a variety of mental experiences and resources. They pleasantly compelled reasoning and creating—started the unquenchable imagination. In a short time a child was telling of his interests, talking about his experiences. He was learning; he had begun to create and to express. He was interested in life.

Doctor Arnold said that if he could teach his boys but one thing, "that thing would be poetry." Poetry, of course, sustains and develops that strange but almost all masterly faculty called imagination. And it is doubtful that any influence so helps the imagination as the influence of nature on the child's mind. When Captain Scott was dying in the Antarctic ice fields he wrote to Mrs. Scott: "Make our boy interested in natural history if you can."

Agassiz has said that a year or two of natural history would give the best kind of training for any other sort of mental work.

Long ago Tyndall emphasized the fact that first-hand facts and materials are infinitely more valuable than those brought to us. Burbank has repeatedly said that intimate contact with nature is necessary for children.

A trail school may be had anywhere. In any nook where nature reigns she tells her story to all children brought to her and they hear her enthusiastically. A leader or teacher for each school is the rub. Nature will appeal to children and actively interest them unless blocked by the leader.

A witty woman once said that the way to interest children in good books is simply to expose children to them. The chief means of interesting children in nature is to expose them—to bring them into contact with outdoor things. Every child has an inherent interest in the outdoors, which with a little tact may be tied up with any other interest desired—books, a specialty, or with any and every phase of life.

What I wish to bring out particularly does not concern the enrichment of botanical and zoological knowledge, greatly important as I regard this, but rather the enlarging and liberalizing influences which Nature has on the public mind generally.

—Dr. William E. Ritter.

A Day with a Nature Guide

One morning six variously attired people, four men and two women, started from a hotel in the Rocky Mountain National Park with a nature guide. An auto whirled them to the end of the road far up the mountainside from whence they continued afoot. They were bound for one of the eternal snowdrifts on Long's Peak.

The essence of nature guiding is to travel gracefully rather than to arrive. This guide tactfully put two or three at ease by convincing them that in the United States the belief in ferocious animals is a superstition. "And no one," he continued, "in this locality has ever been attacked by a wild animal." The day was perfect, but so interestingly did the guide describe experiences in storms that everyone hoped to be Rain-in-the-Face before evening.

The guide was jollied for being silent. These people, true to the customs of the day, asked for rubberneck specialties and demanded where their megaphone artist was. They were climbing in a V-shaped canyon, traveling west. Presently the guide pointed out that the right or north wall rises steeply in the sun and is covered with a scattered growth of stocky, long-armed pines. The left or south wall, which faces north, has a crowded growth of short-armed, tall spruces. In the bottom of the canyon between these closely approaching, but unlike forests is a lively stream with a few accompanying firs, willows, and flowers.

Each member of the party remembered something of plant distribution and each contributed something to the discussion concerning plant zones, slope exposures, temperature, and moisture—the determinism of ecological influences. When the scraps of information ceased the guide added that each canyon

Enos A. Mills guides a group of librarians.

Enos A. Mills guiding, with his daughter, Enda, on his back.

wall also had its special kinds of insect and mammal life, and that each of these tree species had its peculiar insect enemies and its bird and animal neighbors. Then, too, each individual bird and animal, every pair or flock claimed a small bit of territory and commonly lived closely within this, likewise insisting on neighbors keeping within their own reservation.

The nature guide is at his best when he discusses facts so that they appeal to the imagination and to the reason, gives flesh and blood to cold facts, makes life stories of inanimate objects. He deals with principles rather than isolated information, gives biographies rather than classifications. People are out for recreation and need restful, intellectual visions, and not dull, dry facts, rules, and manuals. What the guide says is essentially nature literature rather than encyclopedia natural history.

This party being interested in the distribution of plant and animal life, and in erosion, the guide made these the features of the day's excursion. In a mountain region widely varying life zones are seen side by side; and two or three types of erosion may, in places, be seen from one viewpoint—the wear and tear on the earth's surface by many forces stands out unmistakably.

All that the guide said concerning erosion could be set down under the heading: The Biography of a Canyon. The various forces of erosion—running water, frost, ice, and acid, each at work in its respective place with distinctive tools—were prying, wedging, cutting the canyon wider and deeper. Roots wedged the rocks and dissolved them with acids, but at the same time helped also to resist these tireless forces, placing a binding, holding network of fibers. Gravity handled the transportation of dislodged material.

Each species of plant and animal is of orderly distribution and is found in the places that furnish it the necessities of life. On the middle slopes of the Rocky Mountains are trees, flowers, and animals that are not found a thousand feet farther up the slopes or down the slopes a thousand feet in the foothills. The guide's discussion was the autobiography of each species—The Story of My Life, or How I Came to Be Where I Am and What I Am. In this each plant and animal gave its adventures, its customs, its home territory, its climatic zone, and all the endless and insistent play of the radical and romantic forces of evolution, environment, and ecology.

A few popular and scientific names of species were learned but the guide was reticent about giving classifications. His chief aim was to arouse a permanent interest in nature's ways, and this by illuminating big principles.

Climbing silently out of the canyon up a moderate slope just under timberline, this party halted among the trees for a few minutes on the edge of a small, grassy opening. A deer and her two spotted fawns walked out into view, then went across into the woods.

All turned aside and followed a porcupine that was lumbering across the opening, ignoring their presence. The guide remarked that there may have been a time when the porcupine threw his quills, standing up and hurling them, he imagined, like a primitive man a spear, but that the present development of this animal would prevent the quills being thrown more than three or four inches. However, the other woods fellows make it their business to keep out of his way. He has long been known as "the stupidest fellow in the woods": he is the only one who never appears to play, who has no interest in natural history, in nature guides, nor in the world. Being so well shielded and having an inexhaustible food supply in the boundless forests, he has not developed his wit.

Up and on the party went, except a man and woman who lingered to watch porky. In the edge of the woods the guide stopped to wait for the stragglers. But plainly panic-stricken at being separated from the party, they were just disappearing in the woods, headed north. Asking the others not to stir until he returned the guide dashed after them.

On reuniting the party the guide discussed the necessity of all staying together. "Most people," he said, "are easily confused and lose their direction. Thus it is bad for one to forge ahead, or to turn aside, or to stay behind. Moving together is absolutely necessary for the happiness of the party.

"Once," he continued, "a capable fellow said he would go ahead and wait for us at the foot of a nearby cliff. He never reached the cliff. While looking for him others of the party scattered and each and all were lost, and remained out overnight."

A little before noon they walked out of the uppermost edge of the woods among the dwarfed trees and distorted groves at timberline—an aged and battered forest, small and strange. They were above the altitude of eleven thousand feet.

While they were resting the guide called attention to the abundance of paint brush—variously called the painted cup and Indian paint brush—which was growing nearby. "Digging down to the roots of this plant parasite," he said, "you will find the roots of one specimen clasped over the roots of another. Of course its parasitic habits have given in part the form to its leaves and bracts." The mountain climbers at once asked for stories about the character and habits of other flowers and of the trees.

Beyond them on the edge of an Arctic moorland lay a snow-field about two blocks long. It appeared somewhat like uncut marble. Stained with rock dust, inlaid with wind-blown beetles and grasshoppers, its granular material lay melting in the sun. A bright flower border encircled it. It was made up of flowers of many kinds and colors, flowers with and without perfume, flowers dwarfed, and flowers on tall, stately stalks. In small compass was a variety of soil, moisture, and temperature conditions. The soil along the upper edges of the snowfield was course and dry; below, fine and moist. Each species of plants was occupying the peculiar place in which it could best flourish, or from which it could exclude competitors. It was determinism—conditions determining the distribution.

It probably is true that many of these flowers were developed around the Arctic Circle. The guide recounted the great Ice Age story—how plant and bird and animal life had been swept southward by the irresistible, slow-moving glacier. On the mountains the seeds grew, found a home; so, too, the ptarmigan, in conditions somewhat similar to the old home in the Arctic. In this new colony these birds and flowers still maintain the traditions of their respective old families.

"I am disappointed in finding bird life so rare," said one man of the party. "I have seen only one bird this morning." The guide remarked that he had seen at least twelve species of birds, and that directly before them at that moment were three species in plain sight. Why had he seen but a single bird? His eyes had not been trained to see. A day with a nature guide may help to train the eyes and all the senses.

A picnic party usually does much talking and more eating. A sightseeing party often does things by the book and talks by comparison. A botany or a birding party is absorbed in details. But a nature guided party is vastly different from these: all of the party have a broad outdoor interest. They are not in a hurry, they are in a mood to be human. They make intimate friendships while getting acquainted with nature. One day's companionship in the wilds often better acquaints people with each other than years of ordinary association. The members of a nature guided party take on a wider, happier outlook. All are glad to be living.

The Bighorn, or wild mountain sheep, was seen at close range. Why these animals live in the heights among the peaks the year-round is a story that ever stirs. Their scene-commanding, wild environment has exacted of them alertness, positiveness, sharp eyes, and the ability to play safely where there is much space and little substance beneath them. The interest in the lives of these vigorous animals was ever spontaneous. This, like all other subjects, was kept well out of the category of weights and measures; everything that might have been told about the dissected animal was left unsaid; dry bones were not measured, nor the scientific name from the tomb of dead language mentioned.

Knowing the way is now a minor guiding necessity. Mental development and character are the essentials of a successful guide. He needs to have a wide range of knowledge and to be capable of tactfully imparting this directly and indirectly.

The world is beginning to appreciate the necessity of an outside interest. Fortunate is the individual who has a nature hobby. Such an interest is known to improve health, lengthen life, and increase efficiency. An excursion with a nature guide may give any individual a new or a better hobby. Each person receives a chapter in a natural history story that makes him eager for other chapters which he may find anywhere outdoors.

Dr. Liberty H. Bailey strikes the keynote, I think, of nature guiding at a number of points in his "The Nature-Study Idea." At one place in this he says: "I like the man who has had an incomplete course. A partial view, if truthful, is worth more than a complete course, if lifeless. If the man has acquired a power for work, a capability for initiative and investigation, and enthusiasm for the daily life, his incompleteness is his strength. How much there is before him! How eager his eye! How enthusiastic his temper! He is a man with a point of view, not a man with mere facts. This man will see first the large and significant events; he will grasp relationships; he will correlate; later, he will consider the details."

Timberline, what determines it, and the species of trees that compose it; beavers, their part in conservation and their influence on the settlement and exploration of America; parasitic plants; the story of soil; the birth, life, and death of a lake; the home territory of animals; wind, the great seed-sower—are some of the many possible interests of the trail.

A few people for years have practiced nature guiding occasionally. It has made good and it has a place in national life. It carries with it health, mental stimulus, and inspiration. Recently nature guiding was given a definite place in the national parks by the Government licensing a number of nature guides to conduct people through the wilds. Nature ever is liberalizing, and the nature guide is one of the forces moving for the newer education and for the ideal of internationalism.

Nature guiding is not like sightseeing or the scenery habit. The guide sometimes takes his party to a commanding viewpoint or a beautiful spot. But views are incidental. The aim is to illuminate and reveal the alluring world outdoors by introducing determining influences and the respondent tendencies. A nature guide is an interpreter of geology, botany, zoology, and natural history.

This guide listened courteously to those who wanted to display their own information—even to those who indulged in nature-faking or told stories that were whoppers; but he carefully avoided following their example. Local natural history he often related, and he was sure of an interested audience, for everyone enjoys local color and is glad to have past incidents brought to life. He was a true guide. He had the utmost consideration for those in his care, and a quick eye for the interesting and the beautiful. He had the faculty of being entertaining, instructive, watchful, and commanding, all without his party realizing it. He held the climbers together, keeping everyone alert and in good humor; he is doing a distinct and honorable work for the world.

Children enthusiastically enjoy a day with a nature guide and fortunate the child who can have a number of these excursions. They are thought-compelling, interest-arousing. Children are led after the manner of old people. They must not be talked down to. The guide may enter a little more intimately into their joys, perhaps, making slight readjustments to their tastes. As a rule, the imagination of children is more readily and definitely fired than that of older people.

Climbing a high peak is an excellent experience for any child. A thousand movies of mountain climbers, a thousand stories by the climbers themselves, weeks in school, and numerous other experiences cannot do for the child what one day's effort in the heights will do for him. Mountain climbing has rare richness which cannot be transferred, but which any child may make his own in a day.

The climb should be made with a nature guide. One other individual or child might go along, but it would be better for the child to have only the guide to interrupt his stirring thoughts. A day of this kind will do much for the child's imagination and mental resourcefulness, and give a landmark to his mental horizon that will stand out through life.

In this the Age of Movies it will be a fortunate child who has interest in the fundamentals; who is rich through knowing the principles of Nature. An interest in flowers, birds, animals, or geology calls for outdoor excursions, for initiative, gives breadth of view, and is a life-long resource within. The movies will be improved, but even at their best they can never do for a child what an outdoor interest will enable him to do more beneficially for himself.

One day a guide was out with several children under eight years of age. They became interested in a double-topped spruce. They learned that the original treetop was broken off and that the two topmost twigs then bent upward and raced for leadership. They had run a dead heat, as it were, and continued rival leaders. During the remainder of the day the children often spotted a double-topped tree. The cones of trees were noticed, and of course the cones of the balsam fir caused comment because these stood erect upon the limbs instead of hanging down from them.

In a small area, where a forest fire had swept fifteen years before, a few trees had survived. An examination of two of these revealed old fire scars. One of the scars indicated that the tree had been injured by the fire of fifteen years before and by another fire eighty-seven years previous. A few young aspens and thousands of young lodgepole seedlings were starting. Why the lodgepole pines were growing here brought out a discussion concerning the trees that commonly were the first to appear in a cleared or burned-over area. Only a few species of young trees thrive in the sunlight; others need shade in which to start. This principle appealed to the children. An old seed-hoarding lodgepole on the edge of the burned area was surrounded and examined. It had borne a crop of cones each year for seventeen years. All of these cones, unopened, clung thickly over its limbs.

A few days before the guide had led a party of older people over precisely the route followed by these children. He had talked to both parties similarly, but apparently the children had more deep and lasting enjoyment out of the day.

Who would not be delighted to go with a John Burroughs or a John Muir, to be personally conducted to woods, lakes, and streams by anyone who bubbled over with stories about birds, their home life and their travels, chipmunks and their children, and all the other stories and secrets of the wilderness?

It is splendid to have thousands of men, women, and children coming home each year from their vacations talking of the habits and customs of the animals and plants with which they became acquainted on their enjoyable yet purposeful holidays.

Nature guiding need not be confined to national parks. There might well be nature guides in every locality in the land. Fabre has shown monsters and hundreds of little, stirring people cooperating or battling in every growth-filled space. City parks and the wild places near cities and villages are available to thousands of people and are excellent places for the cultural and inspiring excursions with nature guides. Ere long nature guiding will be an occupation of honor and distinction. May the tribe increase!

Elizabeth Frayer Burnell, a Long's Peak Inn guide, speaks to a group on the trail.

We live for the most part in a very iron mask of forms. Our daily ways are at bottom so joyless, so trite, so compulsory, that we must be free and simple sometimes, or we break. Our present world is a world of remarkable civilization and of very superior virtue, but it is not very natural and not very happy. We need yet some snatches of the life of youth—to be for a season simply happy and simply healthy. We need to draw sometimes great drafts of simplicity and beauty. We need sometimes that poetry should be not droned into our ears, but flashed into our senses. And man, with all his knowledge and his pride, needs sometimes to know nothing and to feel nothing but that he is a marvellous atom in a marvellous world.
—Frederic Harrison.

Play and Pranks of Wild Folk

The plays of wild folk are delightful exhibitions and may frequently be enjoyed by those who wait in the wilderness without a gun. Knowing that wild folk play, and that they have a home territory, brings them strangely close to ourselves.

Life in the wild places is not all struggle—not all hunger, fright, and fighting. All wild animals find time to rest, and all from time to time give themselves up to play. They mostly play in silence but a few play noisily; the majority join with others to frolic, but a number of species play singly. Teamwork has an important place in the life of many bird and animal species. And play appears vital to them all.

A tumbleweed in a Wyoming windstorm furnished the plaything in an exciting game for a pack of wolves. I watched the play from the shelter of a ravine. Flying before the wind, the tumbleweed bounded a ridge with a huge wolf leaping after it. Closely pressing him came a pursuing pack of twenty. A lull in the wind and the tumbleweed, colliding with the leading wolf's head, bounded off to one side. Other wolves sprang in the air after it, but the wind carried the tumbleweed along and the entire pack rushed in pursuit.

This big, much-branched, ball-shaped weed was two feet in diameter. When it touched the earth the gale swept it, bounding forward and rolling over and over, across the brown, wide plains. After it came the closely massed wolves. Just as those in the lead were nearing this animated plaything it was caught by a whirlwind and pulled high into the air. Two wolves leaped and tried to seize it. Several sat down and stared after it as though it were gone forever. The tumbleweed commenced to descend, but buoyed up by the air it came down slowly. The pack surged this way and that, as the weed surged in descending, to be beneath it; and while it was still several feet above them a high-leaping fellow struck it head-on and sent it flying to one side. It disappeared in a hollow and the wolves vanished after it. Puffs of dust and occasionally the high-bounding weed itself told me that the game was on as vigorously as ever.

The next act opened with the reappearance of one of the wolves running up a slope and looking back over his shoulder. Up in the wind, a little behind him and off to one side, came the tumbleweed. The wolf turned, leaped at the weed, struck it with his breast, and knocked it vaulting away. The pack, rushing into view, swerved as one to seize or strike it. Each player was intense, and all were as serious as football players. A sweeping gale carried the whirling weed forward again. It came in contact with a rock outcrop and rolled to one side. The whole team rushed at the weed and tumbled pell-mell around it.

In this general mix-up two of the wolves started a fight. The pack joined in the row, struggling and rolling about. A pair occasionally clinched, reared into the air, and fell back. The badly mashed tumbleweed with crippling bounces went on with the wind across the wide, dust-blown plains. Suddenly the fight stopped, the panting wolves stood for a few seconds looking at nothing, then scattered. The play was over. Had it started, I wondered, as unceremoniously, as suddenly, as it stopped?

Most wild animal players are solemn as chess contestants, and most games are as serious as a football match. The characteristic play of the wolf is serious, silent teamwork. But the dignified, independent grizzly plays alone. He, too, romps in silence, but joyfully. He relaxes and has the time of his life. Bears appear to excel in light-hearted, merry make-believe.

A grizzly bear coasting on a steep mountainside made a picturesque play spectacle. He was playing on a summit slope south of Long's Peak in what is now the Rocky Mountain National Park. As he sat down in the snow, put his fore paws on his knees and jiggled himself along to start, he appeared strangely human. At one point he reached back his paw and put on brakes. He ended the coast with a jump and a somersault. Then, selecting a different place on the slope, he started down again, pushing himself along with both fore paws to get up speed. He ended this time by deliberately rolling over and over. Rising on hind feet he looked at his marks on the snowy slope and climbed back up for another coast.

Twice I have seen a black bear, "The Happy Hooligan of the Woods," and a coyote playing together. In one of these games the bear, solemn-looking as an elephant but as merry as a boy, would allow the coyote to leap over him but used his speed and his wits in trying to prevent the coyote from ducking under him or leaping across close in front of him. The coyote's play was puppy-like, though suggesting at times fox cleverness. They were well matched, both in skill and speed. They made lively dashes and swift turns as they raced across a grassy opening in the woods. They varied this swift turning by slow passing, biting, and striking at each other as they met. Then each in turn enjoyed the ludicrous pretense of being asleep while the other went through an equally ludicrous pretense of trying to slip up and surprise the sleeper.

As games often end, this play broke up in a row. The coyote lost his temper and made a fierce but ineffectual attack on the bear. He finally walked off into the woods, with the bear standing looking regretfully after him.

The boy-like black bear would rather play than eat. Once I saw a black bear try repeatedly to get a stupid, lumbering porcupine to play with him. All the way across an opening he made efforts to start a game, but dull porky lumbered on indifferently. The porcupine is the only animal that I have known which I have never seen play.

The black bear will play with bears, or with other animals, or with people with apparently equal enjoyment. In the Yellowstone

I raced and dodged about with several that were nearly wild, to my own entertainment as well as theirs. Bears play less often with objects. I once watched a make-believe battle which one was having with a stump, and on another occasion I saw an older bear with a cone, striking it about, tossing it into the air, trying to catch it as it fell, and shaking it in his teeth as he rolled about on his back with feet in the air.

In most cases neither birds nor animals use playthings. But I have seen birds play with sticks, stones, leaves, and nuts; an otter play with shells and even using a live turtle for a plaything; and a grizzly playing with a floating log.

Rambling through the Medicine Bow Mountains of Colorado one afternoon, I came upon a grizzly bear sitting on his haunches like a dog and looking with all attention across a beaver pond. Making a quiet detour through the primeval forest I found that he was watching a number of otter playfully coasting on their slide.

The smooth, slippery, wet slide, about forty feet long, came down the steeply wooded slope into the south shore of the pond. The slide was well worn and testified to the strong play habits of these animals. Each coasting otter ended with a merry splash as he slid into the water. The glimpses that I had of the coasters showed that they were all enjoyment. The grizzly, all the time I watched, was giving the otter enthusiastic attention. But he was only one of many spectators. A flock of wild ducks sat motionless in the pond observing the players. The coasting suddenly stopped and the otter disappeared in the water. A squirrel on a spruce limb overhanging the slide had also been a wondering spectator of the play, and with jerky, hesitating chatter of a bark expressed his disappointment and disapproval because the performance was ended.

The characteristic play of coyotes is noisy. They have concerts full of howls, barks, and yelps, in ever-varying combinations. These players have regular places for assembling and both singly and collectively send their wild notes flying at different angles off into the night. There are weird, ventriloquial effects which sometimes multiply and reproduce one yapping, yelping entertainer into a scattered number. At other times the howler so transfers his voice that it seems to issue from a point widely separated from the owner. Sometimes this clown of the prairie forgets singing to the stars, and in silence has games and contests which require speed and skill.

The humpback whale appears to be the most playful fellow of the seven seas. He plays singly, with other whales of all ages, and he will even play with a ship. Off the coast of Alaska a number of humpbacks were at play near the steamer on which I was a passenger. They appeared to have great fun. As speedy and as agile as trout, they threshed about, raced, and countermarched. One literally stood on his head, and with only his tail out of the water beat and churned the waves violently. Most of all they appeared to enjoy diving, then coming to the surface with all possible speed, shooting thirty or more feet of their ponderous bodies out of the water, and rolling awkwardly to one side as they fell heavily back into the sea.

The play of the jays and the crows is often fun at the expense of others. Clarke's nutcracker is a rowdy, assailing squirrels and precipitating fights between birds of other species. He is also a daredevil in flying exhibitions and excels in spectacular airplane dips.

The long crested jay is keen witted and cynical, and it seems natural that in playing he should go the limit in rowdyism and the ridiculous, and indulge in endless pranks. He is strong for vaudeville and farces; he likes to impersonate, to surprise, and to annoy. I once saw a number of jays in an exhibition in which each seemed to be endeavoring to outdo the others. They skipped and jumped, kicked awkwardly, caricatured the pose of a stork, somersaulted, and tried flying from a height with one wing and dropping ungracefully upside down—no end of reckless rowdyism and mockery.

Once in the snow on a mountain top I saw a flock of ptarmigan in a strange, energetic, though silent, dance. Most birds are quiet in their play.

Four sedate and wise old owls surprised me beyond measure with a play that was mostly ridiculous showing off. They tried to do a few things absurdly impossible for them to do. One of these stunts was chasing their tails, and another was high kicking. But

Enos A. Mills and his daughter, Enda, by a stream.

most of their efforts were more in keeping with their ordinary mien; they bowed profoundly, they posed in lordly pairs, they looked to the right and left with a most aristocratic air, they adjusted and readjusted themselves with ceremonious dignity.

The energetic beaver gives marked attention to play. Each summer he has a vacation of three months or longer. He probably loafs the most of any animal in the wilds. He plays much and often and is master of the fine art of rest.

Although I have seen mountain lions only a few times when they were not frightened, twice I watched them play. On one of these occasions the lion was enjoying the pretense of running down an animal, and carried out a lively pantomime in the snow, frolicking like a kitten.

One spring day a flock of Bighorn sheep found a large snowdrift across their trail on the summit of Storm Pass. They could easily have gone around it, but evidently saw here what suggested an excuse to frolic. One at a time, they started to jump the drift. The first performer, on gaining the farther side, turned about to watch the others try it. As each jumper landed he quickly lined up with those who had preceded him and faced about to watch the performance, while the sheep awaiting their turn also gave their close attention as each jump was made.

The style of jump and the distance covered were much alike in each case. Most of the sheep made a standing jump; two or three backed off several steps and got a running start for the leap. One made a clumsy pretense of slipping and came down in the snow on his side. Two young lambs went together and instead of jumping far, jumped high, coming down in the center of the drift. After the last one had crossed the sheep stood together for a few seconds and then strolled on, plainly with nothing in particular to do.

One day I saw a number of sheep scrambling and circling on an icy slope. The fun probably was to keep from falling, but it may have been in the falling. Every one fell a number of times. A few times all four feet shot from beneath a sheep at once, and in his sliding a number of rising efforts were made, only to result in the sheep's falling each time before it got on its feet again.

Even butterflies play. Climbers on Long's Peak sometimes see them floating up the Trough. Often there is an air current flowing up the Trough, and sometimes this catches hats and takes them with it.

One calm, sunny day I looked down over the summit of the Peak and saw a procession of butterflies floating or sailing up the Trough. On reaching the summit a majority of them dropped down the vertical south wall of the Peak about four hundred feet, then flew westward and swung in behind a pinnacle where they reentered the Trough near the bottom. At a point where an upstanding rock in the Trough changed the current there was a lively flapping of wings as though these aviators, like boatmen in rapids, were tensely concentrated. Rarely did a butterfly leave the ranks in ascending, though in coming down the line was more broken.

It was a wild region for these fragile-winged creatures. The first time that I saw them I long watched and wondered what it was all about. After seeing similar exhibitions elsewhere, and after watching repeated flights at this place, I concluded that butterflies, as well as other life, play.

On perfect days butterflies sail over high moorlands and even cross high mountain tops. But while sailing on the heights they are ever vigilant for wind. The short-lived, unannounced gusts would blow their tender wings to pieces in an instant. If a dash of wind, or sometimes just a cloud shadow comes, they fold wings and drop to the earth. There they lie motionless until all danger is passed. Yet these frail, afraid-of-the-wind people seek out a place of their liking to play high up among the crags.

I recall once having seen two different plays going on side by side. Each was a stirring glimpse of motherhood. A mother bear lay on her side contentedly watching the cubs as they wrestled, boxed each other, and occasionally mauled her. They were near the summit of the Continental Divide and all around were scattered snowdrifts and aged, storm-battered pines. On a nearby Cliff were a bighorn ewe and two lambs. The lambs were leaping over the mother and playing with each other. Each wild mother knew of the other's presence, but was indifferent.

With animals, as with ourselves, play appears to be necessary

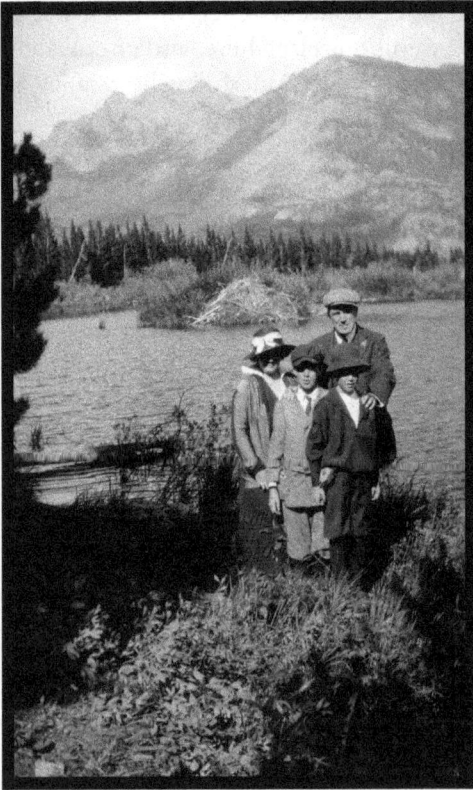

This page: George Horace Lorimer with his family at the Moraine Beaver Colony.

for the development of the young and for the sustained fitness of the mature. As a factor which gives success, it probably ranks with food and sleep. Play drills give development and efficiency.

Play is the nearest approach to the magic fountain of youth. Distinguished wild folk, those alert and quick to readjust themselves to the ever-changing conditions—those surviving, succeeding and evolving—are those ever loyal to life's best ally—the youth called Play.

The wonderful story of Evolution shows that playing animals are most likely to survive and leave offspring. Cooperation or teamwork appears to be the outgrowth of team play. This is closely allied to Mutual Aid, which is a conspicuous factor in Evolution, and in Mutual Aid appears to be the beginning of a conscious consideration for the rights of others.

To speak about sparing anything because it is beautiful is to waste one's breath and incur ridicule in the bargain. The aesthetic sense—the power to enjoy through the eye, the ear, and the imagination—is just as important a factor in the scheme of human happiness as the corporeal sense of eating and drinking; but there has never been a time when the world would admit it. The "practical men," who seemed forever on the throne, know very well that beauty is only meant for lovers and young persons—stuff to suckle fools withal. The main affair of life is to get the dollar, and if there is any money in cutting the throat of beauty, why, by all means, cut her throat. That is what "practical men" have been doing since the world began.

—Dr. John C. Van Dyke.

Censored Natural History News

The Ancients went in strong for superstitions both in peace and war. These were supposedly for the general welfare. The pagan priests in power during the closing days of old Rome are said never to have met without laughing over the observed superstitions which they were perpetuating. One of the greatest victories recorded for a Roman admiral was the sinking of a superstition. He was about to meet the fleet of the enemy for a decisive of battle when the sacred chickens aboard refused to eat. This bad omen discouraged the superstitious sailors, and even the officers were losing their morale. The admiral, however, promptly threw the chickens overboard, with the remark that perhaps they would drink, and proceeded to victory.

A story of modern origin and common circulation has the Bighorn mountain sheep dive over precipices and triumphantly land on his horns at the bottom. The Bighorn does not know this story and the plan is strange to him. The few sheep that may have tried it never returned to report results.

Dall DeWees, the world-wide naturalist and hunter, has another sheep story. He sat behind a newspaper near a hotel group who were telling hunting incidents and discussing alleged natural history. It was too much for him when someone told how the Bighorn mountain sheep use their horns for shock-absorbers. He quietly interrupted with: "Gentlemen, I had a Bighorn sheep experience near my mountain home. Walking along the bottom of the deep, narrow Arkansas River canyon one day a few bits of granite fell at my feet. I saw on the upper rim a number of mountain sheep, and as I looked up the leader, an old ram, dived over." Here Dall paused and someone wanted to know what became of the sheep. "Oh," said Mr. DeWees, "he saw me and turned around and went back."

Without a knowledge of natural history a person with a gun is likely to get his wild life classifications wrong and take a shot at something out of season. Once I was quietly watching a dignified social gathering of pelicans in a pond when a hunter from the rear took a crack at me. He made haste to apologize with the explanation that he mistook me for a goose.

Those who are not up on wilderness etiquette have gossiped most unfairly about the skunk. First of all, he is ever ready for society, his company manners in constant use—never mislaid; he is well groomed; makes no advances unless introduced; and he meets visitors face to face. The skunk ever acts nicely except when jostled; the intruder and the impolite he endeavors to sterilize or screen off with clean chemical spray.

Every wild thing under the sun seems to have suffered from the censorship of nature news. Geese are supposed to be stupid and loons crazy, but both are exceptionally keen-witted. The misstatements from which they and the skunk suffer satisfy only the censor and some others.

This censorship of natural history news, begun a few generations ago, has developed to near exclusiveness of facts. Those censoring appear wholly unacquainted with their subject, and therefore are qualified by censor tests to give the public such selected nature lore as it can be trusted to know and still remain loyal to public institutions. A Scottish philosopher once said that history is a set of lies agreed upon. Natural history as it is now censored is an excellent example of the stifling possibilities of censorship.

A number of people in California and Australia have been watching for a frightened ostrich to hide his head in the sand. It is

The first snow before the frost.

Looking over Trail Ridge,
Rocky Mountain National Park.

possible that a mentally deranged plume-bearer may yet be discovered who will do this. But it has never been considered good form among the common run of ostriches.

Dan Beard, in a youthful sketching effort, sat down before a flock of Florida ostriches. They became curious at his general appearance and concentration and two came and looked over his shoulder. He has never exhibited the picture. Possibly it was of an ostrich hiding its lamps ungracefully in a bushel of sand. Anyway, they looked and were agitated, but, instead of hiding their heads, chased Dan ingloriously down street; they routed him; helmet and all the equipment were thrown away to aid flight for safety first. Ever since this experience Dan Beard has done pioneer work in natural history and has called the nature censor everything but a gentleman.

Going into the wild places is too often considered akin to joining the suicide club because wild animals are thought to be ferocious, altitude almost as dangerous, while storms and lightning make the outdoors a continuous battlefield. Yet the wilderness is the safety zone of the world. It postpones the death of practically all its visitors.

One of the most encouraging and significant tendencies of the times is the growing distrust of the censor of natural history news. He is becoming unpopular and may have to take to the woods and learn something. People are responding to the call of the wild. In increasing numbers they are going far in wild places, returning one hundred percent fit from top to toe; with enthusiastic morale they condemn the molly-coddle doctrine and the evil propaganda of the natural history censors.

The Boy Scouts and the Campfire Girls are endangering the natural history censor. These healthy youngsters will give intelligent determinism to future natural history. Dragonflies will have to cease being "Devil's darning-needles," toads stop producing warts, fuzz will have to function otherwise than keeping plants warm in winter. If one beaver colony forecasts a hard winter and another in the same locality plans for a mild one, both will be allowed to do so uncensored, and if porcupines go about the woods throwing their quills like bushmen their boomerangs, something will happen to them, too. With a little more general acquaintance with wild life and woodcraft there will be an open season on censors.

Prairie dogs live in arid lands. For weeks their only water is that from plants eaten. There is a story of general circulation which tells that prairie-dog holes go down to water. Oil and artesian wells in prairie-dog towns show that the depth to water is from two hundred to five hundred feet, a depth impossible for the prairie dog, but not for the storyteller. Although, too, the chief concern of Mrs. Prairie Dog is to prevent snakes eating her young, the story goes out that snakes, prairie dogs, and owls live happily in the same hole.

Roosevelt has commented on the superstitions concerning the alleged ferocity of American animals in general and the mountain lion in particular. He brought forward first-hand experience and an array of competent witnesses to show that the lion or puma does not leap from tree limbs onto people, that it is an extremely shy animal, and that one is as safe sleeping in its territory as among tame cats; and, he might have added, much less likely to be disturbed.

That fear of snakes, sharks, and devilfish probably have sentenced more people to close confinement than is commonly known. It discourages views afoot. The devilfish has been the villain of ten thousand adventure stories, yet it does not seek human prey. The shark, too, is a magical find for many an inaccurate scribbler.

Snakes are not so big nor so bad nor so common as nursery news proclaims. There are two evil and impossible snake stories that appear to have circulated for generations in Asia, Europe, Africa, and America. At present they are infesting the tourist routes in South America as thickly as snakes in a booze nightmare. One of these stories has a snake so large that he swallows an ox, tail foremost, and comes to grief when the long, out-pointing horns are reached. This story is sometimes varied by describing a snake with the shoulders, body, and horns of an ox, and a tail more than one hundred feet long. The most stretched snake skin ever exhibited was only twenty-five feet long.

Some years ago an alleged sea serpent—made in Germany—

was exhibited to crowds in the capitals of Europe. Taking the skull of one and most of the bones of several ancient Zeuglodons, the inventor multiplied the real length and exhibited the combination as one 114-foot skeleton. Sea serpents, if they ever existed, are extinct; but the "Petrified Man," too, still draws crowds although no petrified man has ever been discovered.

The wolves of the United States have not been ferocious for generations, if ever so. Their keen senses are ever alert to avoid coming close to people and in keeping out of sight. Yet a number of times each year telegrams appear in the newspapers telling of an attack of wolves on people. Such accounts discourage outdoor life and help keep natural history safe for hypocrisy. The following was printed in a newspaper in February, 1919:

"Wolves are attacking children on their way home from school in my country and have treed people, keeping them in trees all night...They attack men and are killing sheep, cattle, and hogs. One man recently saved his life by killing a wolf after it had jumped into a sleigh in which the man was riding."

The cow for story purposes is more picturesque than the grizzly bear. How interesting it might be if someone would write a story of the capers of a cow that chased strangers up trees then climbed after them! Such a story might be justified as a work of art and the author honored as a clever entertainer, but the fact remains that neither the cow nor the grizzly bear climbs trees.

"Working like a beaver" is a proverb sometimes applied to people, with complement intended. It is interpreted to mean great industry—working all the time and overtime but not necessarily accomplishing anything or having a goal.

The life of the beaver is rich in edifying material, but the preachments and morals concerning his life appear to have been made mostly by censors and professional uplifters without the golden facts. Their pointing to the beaver for lessons and teachments in the world of nature would not be so bad if they called attention to actualities. The beaver ever has a purpose; he never works unless he has to do so, this is possibly one day out of seven; he is efficient; and, although his accomplishments are monumental, he is master of the fine art of rest.

A dozen scouts and leader camped last winter for a week in the mountains. They tried to discover what the groundhog did on Groundhog Day. Would the groundhogs, mindful of their vast responsibilities, come forth or thrust out their heads to announce the weather for the next sixty days? The scouts were in the woods owned by the father of one of the boys who knew the location of many groundhog holes. Twelve of these were marked and watched. Four holes were drifted over, sealed with snow, but Mr. Groundhog did not break a seal; five others were partly filled with snow, but evening came and this snow received not a track, the hibernating hog hibernated on; at two of the other three holes nothing showed up; but midafternoon, cheering in the direction of the third caused the twelve scouts quickly to collect. A cottontail rabbit had put out his head, looked toward every point on the horizon and at the sky, and then had gone back! For these Boy Scouts the weather will hereafter have to be regulated without a groundhog. Perhaps some day the Scouts will look into prairie dog holes.

The object of the censors seems to have been to keep people indoors, to keep them from knowing the facts about natural history and the outdoors. It is but little less than a crime to attempt to suppress a normal child who has become restless through indoor life by telling him that bears eat bad children. Bears never eat human flesh.

Nor are bears ferocious. Bears, like all strong and desirable citizens, are constantly assailed with attempts at character assassination. People who are constantly maligning the bear probably do not have anything against him, but he simply is their favourite factor for trying to accomplish a purpose through fear. They believe that people can be frightened into doing what indoor folk considered good, like staying indoors and other debatable conventions. Punishments and threats were in vogue during the Dark Ages, when education was discounted and kings and powers-that-be sought service and servility.

However, there appears to be an open season on superstitions. Ghosts are almost exterminated. Witches on broomsticks will need to watch their way where Liberty Motors fly. Many alleged man-eating monsters and monstrosities are already as dead as Dinosaurs. The increasing numbers of wild life reservations and the enlarged numbers of people who have met bears and wolves face to face will, ere long, cast animal superstitions and the divine right of kings into the scrap heap of models that have had their day.

Many wild animals appear to have courage, conscience, and common sense. Often they triumph over the unexpected, quickly they readjust to new conditions, sometimes they welcome reform, and often they cooperate and combine for the general welfare.

Why make the wilderness a fearful place, full of ferocious beasts and dangerous forces? No nation has fallen for fostering outdoor life. Indoor excesses have covered the outdoors with superstitions and closed doors against the enjoyment of invigorating storms and snows. Every season has its advantages. Forgetting that change and winter of temperate zone gave vigor and courage to the race, the exclusive indoor peoples have missed and lost much that is good. The changes that challenge and compel growth and keep us fit and growing, these give the required and necessary morale for those in life's front ranks. At times the Old Acquaintance has been stern, but it raised and conducted our distinguished ancestors to us, and for those who don't forget there is renewed health and hope—the world is young once more.

The wild wonderlands give to every child that guiding and glorious light—imagination. Wild nature is the child's greatest heritage. Unfortunately superstitions and system do not know this shining heritage and this wondrous light many a child will never see.

"Mother," said a small boy, as they stood before the leopard's cage, "how can that animal afford a coat like yours?"

This childish remark is akin to the lofty condescension sometimes observed in the comments concerning the rural population. People, without knowledge, allege inferiority in rural folk. Country folk and the farmer are thought to be in need of uplift and old magazines.

Many wilderness camping places are devastated as though by war. Trees are burned and hacked, birds shot and frightened, and wild flowers uprooted. These atrocities are committed by those who have a low estimate of poetic wild nature, of everything and everybody beyond the city limits. But these people are not to blame. Their early nature information was misinformation. The Scouts are already showing that nature censorship is in Class A of nonessentials.

Much of Roosevelt's power came from early—that is, correct—acquaintance with nature; it furnished him recreation and enjoyment and efficiency; and it also stored his mind with inside facts which ever were helpful in making the right decision and in getting results.

Some years ago a lumber company endeavoured to acquire a large block of timberland from the Government. President Roosevelt, doubting either the correctness of the representations of the company concerning the character of the timber, or desiring to reserve the area, denied the application. Later he reopened the case and the manager of the company came on for the final statement. During the discussion the manager exhibited photographs alleged to be the tract in question.

The leading photograph was marked: "Engelmann spruce on southern slope of Granite Mountain, altitude 7,000 feet." Roosevelt at once asked concerning the accuracy of the legend. The manager doubly assured him of its absolute accuracy. Roosevelt knew spruce and other tree habits and habitats in the locality represented, and realized that the Engelmann spruce was found mostly on cool northern, not warm southern slopes, and at the altitude of 9,000 feet or more, and not, as a legend said, at 7,000 feet.

People are made in their leisure hours. It is insidious enemy propaganda which discourages the best use of leisure hours— outdoor exercise—and encourages indoor functions as the conventional thing. Functions have been tried by many people who have ceased to be fit, to have morale; and by many a nation which no longer has a place in the sun.

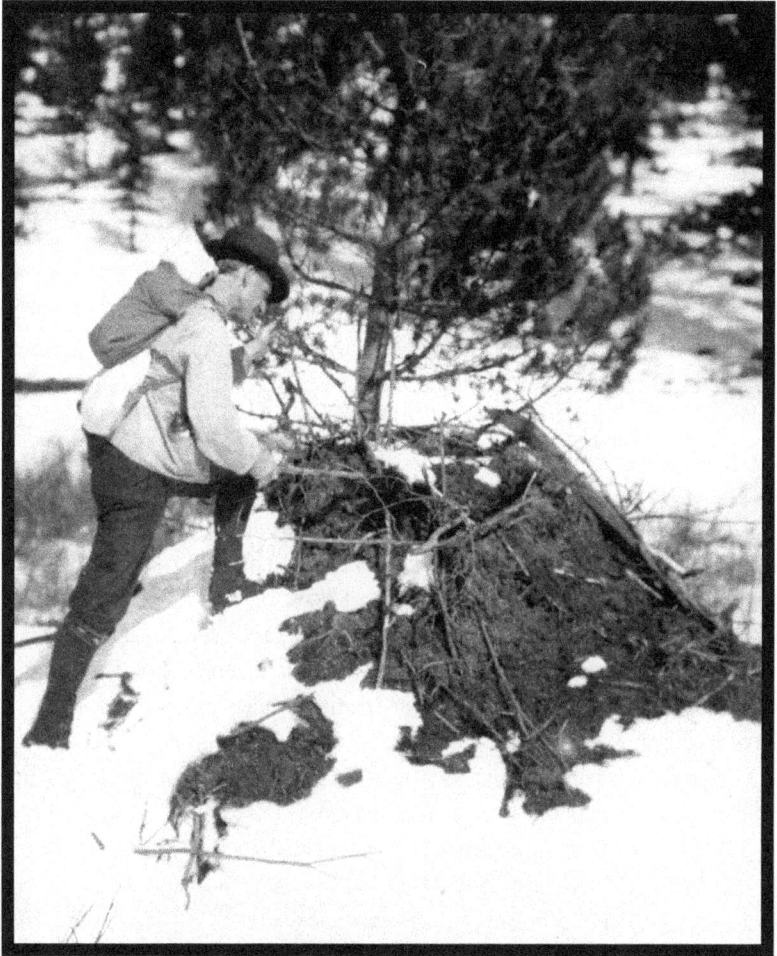

Enos A. Mills inspects a beaver house,
with his daughter, Enda, on his back.

American schools have, as a matter of fact, failed to train the great mass of the children for successful earning of a livelihood in the American world of today, and at the same time they have failed, for the most part, to inspire the children with the tastes, ambitions, and aspirations which would guide them to a sensible and enjoyable use of their leisure.
                    —Dr. Charles W. Eliot.

Harriet—Little Mountain Climber

Little Harriet Peters, a six-year-old friend of mine, was listening intently to the comments of the climbers whom I had just guided to the summit of Long's Peak. They were describing their trip to a number of others. Presently Harriet turned to me and asked what birds and animals lived on the top of this high peak of the Rockies.

Often I had been asked what could be seen from the top of the Peak; many people were curious about the size of the summit; most interested climbers wanted to know how long it took to go up and back; but never before had anyone asked what lived there.

When the mountain climbing discussion ended this little girl very soberly asked if I would sometime take her to the top of Long's Peak.

"Yes," I replied, "just as soon as we feel that you can go up and back easily. It is a long, steep climb."

Then she wanted to know: "Is it uphill all the way?"

I had early become interested in Harriet, she was so alert, so quiet, and always so cheerful and wide awake. She often went off alone to climb the nearby trails, or for a ride on her burro. Of course she enjoyed playing with other children. Though she had never been to school she had learned to read, and every day out of doors she appeared to be learning new things.

She was constantly surprising me by asking a lively and original question which showed that she saw many of the interesting things around her and wondered about them.

"How do beavers sharpen their teeth?" she asked one day. We had returned a few hours before from a visit to a beaver colony,

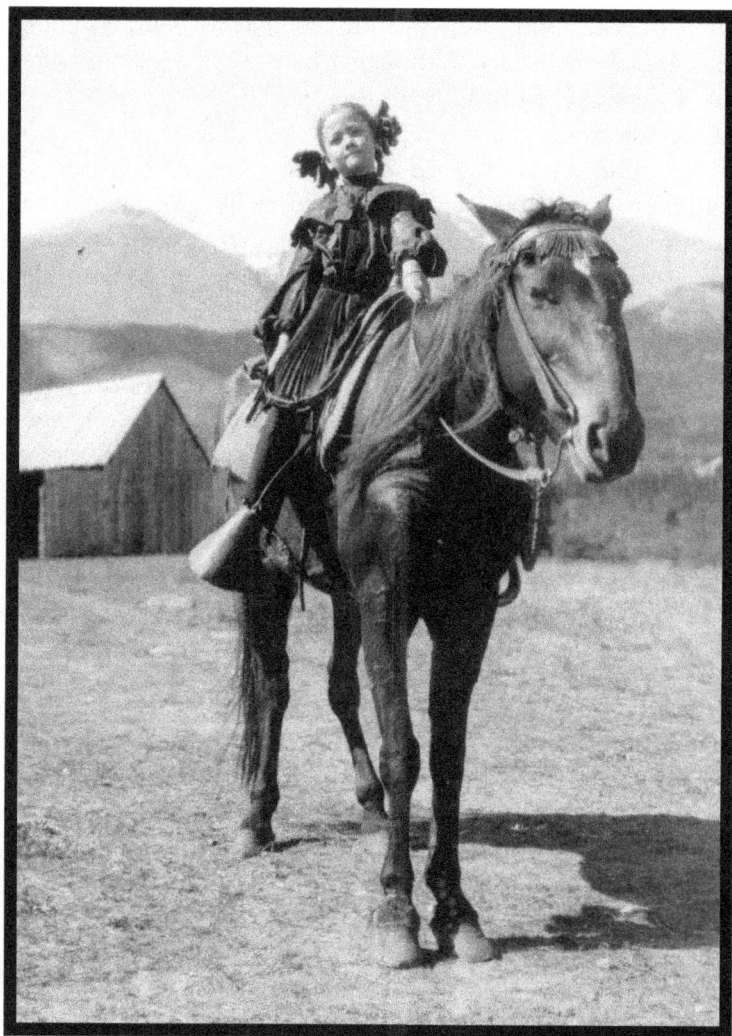

Harriet Peters on her way up Long's Peak.

where we had seen in number of large, dead trees whose hard wood showed the marks of the beavers' gnawing.

Harriet really wanted to get on top of Long's Peak; she was curiously, thoughtfully interested in the things to be seen on the summit of this rocky, snowy landmark that towered so grandly 14,255 feet into the sky. Although I had never taken anyone so young I was eager to go up with her.

One autumn day, just after Harriet was eight years of age, we went up. We started off on horseback. The trail begins in a mountain valley, 9,000 feet above sea level. The Peak rises in the sky one mile higher. After galloping a short distance we walked our ponies so that they might breathe for a stretch before taking another gallop. Harriet wanted to know why it was we slowed down when we might have galloped to the steeper part of the trail. Why I tightened the saddle cinches also called for an explanation.

"A person who walks with a loose shoe receives a blistered foot, and a horse ridden with a loose saddle receives a blistered back," I told her.

Most of the time Harriet was silent, observing, and thoughtful, but occasionally she asked a definite question about the things nearby. She was interested in the new and unusual objects along the way. The lodgepole pine, perhaps because of its name, caused her to ask many questions. She wanted to know if Arkansas pine, such trees as she saw in her Arkansas home, also lived in the Rocky Mountains. She asked the name of the trees growing in groups near the lively brook along which we were riding. These were young balsam fir trees and the purple cones that stood upon the topmost limbs not far above her head attracted her attention.

She had remembered hearing that up the mountainside there were species of trees that did not live in the valley, and that at timberline, where the forest edge is farthest up the mountain, lives still other kinds of trees. While traveling westward in a canyon I pointed out the scattered limber pines growing on the north wall, in the sun, and the dense, tall growth of Engelmann spruce on the shady, opposite wall. She was interested that these two kinds of trees were living so close together, and yet one species kept on the warmer, drier side of the canyon and the other on the cooler, moister slope, while the firs grew only along the stream.

We saw a number of chipmunks eating the scarlet berries of the low-growing kinnikinick. They allowed us to ride close to them, and appeared so tame that Harriet asked:

"If we had time to stop would they let me play with them like the chipmunks around your cabin?"

The night before had been stormy on the upper mountain slopes. Harriet was surprised that there were a few inches of snow here and none down below. She was riding ahead that she might better see the fresh tracks of the birds and animals in the trail. There were many rabbit tracks clean-cut and splashed. It looked as though they had had a game. Suddenly my pony bumped into Harriet's who had stopped and turned to ask:

"Have some bare-footed children and their mother been up the trail this morning?"

A line of big tracks came out of the woods on the left and followed the trail up the mountain. How strangely like the tracks of bare-footed children and an old person; the tracks of a mother bear and two cubs! Slowly, quietly, not even whispering, we rode up the mountain hoping to see them. We were scolded by a pine squirrel for moving so cautiously. We saw where the bears had eaten blueberries in the snow; but there were no bears.

At timberline, 11,000 feet above sea level, all of the trees were small; yet they did not look like young trees, but appeared aged, storm-beaten, and strange. Many of them really were hundreds of years old, yet so tiny that Harriet could reach to the top of them. Many were not so tall as she.

"My doll would like to climb them but they are too small for me to climb," she said.

We tied our ponies and rambled along this strange edge of the forest. There were pines, firs, spruces, dwarfed birch and aspen, and Arctic willow.

"Why," Harriet asked, "do these little people live up here on the cold mountainside?"

Magpies, camp-birds, and Clarke's nutcrackers were numerous, having a nutting picnic. All were having great fun, but the nutcrackers were getting most of the nuts, pecking holes in the pine cones, and busily eating the large, almost ripened fruit, and calling noisily. One of the camp-birds alighted upon Harriet's shoulder, curious to know if she had something for him to eat. They are perhaps the most sociable and the best-known birds in the western mountains.

About nine o'clock the sun came out and the snow began to melt. The remainder of the day was calm and warm. No air stirred. On the Arctic moorlands above the timberline we watched carefully, hoping to see the Bighorn. We did not see even the track of one. But we came up on a flock of ptarmigan. These birds had already laid off most of their light brown summer clothes and were dressed in almost pure white.

The last three miles of the seven steep, winding miles to the summit are entirely above the limits of tree growth, among rocky crags and old snowfields, with most of the trail over either solid or broken rock.

On Boulderfield, five miles from our starting point, we tied our ponies to rocks in the shelter of large boulders and continued upward on foot. Harriet was a sure-footed climber. As we started across this mile stretch of glacial moraine I told her that expert mountaineers travel slowly, always look before making a step, and stopped for talking or looking around. Occasionally we rested, and sometimes we lay down upon a flat boulder and thoroughly relaxed.

At about 13,000 feet, while we were thus resting, became a strange, chirpy squeak. Harriet heard it repeated a number of times before asking what it was. Presently a little animal resembling a rabbit somewhat, but more nearly like a guinea pig, ran in front of us, carrying in its mouth a few blades of course grass and one or two tiny Arctic plants. It was the mountain cony.

"Was he squealing because someone bit his ears off?" Harriet asked. The cony's short ears do appear as though clipped.

I told her that the cony is called the "hay maker of the heights"; each autumn he gathers small haycocks of plants and stores them among the boulders for his winter food.

"Why doesn't he go down the mountain and live by the brook where there is more hay?" Was another question that I could not answer.

About a thousand feet below the top of the Peak we turned aside for a drink from a tiny spring, the last water on the way up. Here we lingered several minutes. Harriet gathered a double handful of snow and carried it to the spring that she might send more water down the Mississippi to New Orleans. Then of the wet snow she made a dam on the rocks where the water flowed from the spring.

Leaving this place we did steep rock climbing over a few hundred feet to the Narrows. In places Harriet walked in front of me; but most of the time she was behind, and always close. By listening carefully I could tell that all was well with her without looking back. At no time were we roped together. In a few places I helped her, but most of the time she walked alone.

A few snowdrifts and ice-piles remain on the head and shoulders of the Peak all summer. The upper two thousand feet is almost solid rock; there are cracks, ledges, and shattered places, with a pinnacle and shattered rock around its base. Here and there was a beauty spot—a tiny bed of soil covered with grass and flowers in the midst of rocky barrenness.

From the Narrows, a little below the summit, we saw two eagles soaring and circling about in the air two or three thousand feet above us. A few times their shadows dashed by us. The Narrows is a ledge, a shelf-like stretch of trail, on the edge of a precipice. There is no bannister here, but one is needed. Many grown people have stopped at this point, but Harriet walked across without saying a word.

Up the "Homestretch"—the last climb to the top—the slope is extremely steep and the rock solid. Here many people call out "safety first" and go up on all fours, but Harriet, who was in front of me, walked up swinging her arms and humming softly to herself.

We arrived at the summit of the Peak a little after twelve o'clock, five hours from the time we started. The broken summit surface is nearly level, and strewn with slabs and angular chunks of pink granite, from sand and coarse gravel up to blocks several feet across. The instant we stepped on the top I said to Harriet:

"Now you are here, what do you think of it?"

She stood for nearly a minute looking around without saying a word, then asked:

"Where did all the rocks come from?"

Harriet was surprised to find the top so large. There was just about room to give all the players in a baseball game place to stand, with the batter, first baseman, and outfielders all standing on the edge. We walked around the top, keeping close to the edge. In most places it dropped off steeply for a hundred feet. The east side is a perpendicular wall more than a thousand feet high. There were many cracked and loose stones on the edge; many were almost ready to fall overboard, as numerous others had already done. Plainly the top of the Peak had once been much larger. Just as we were sitting down to eat our lunch Harriet asked:

"How big was the top once?"

We sat in a safe place near the edge of a precipice where we could look down into Chasm Lake—a glacier-made basin—2,000 feet below us. The water, though clear, appeared as green as any emerald ink you have ever seen.

A half-tamed groundhog, that in summer lived upon the summit, came forth to have scraps of our lunch. A flock of rosy finches alighted near us. A hummingbird flew over without stopping. A number of butterflies circled about in the calm, sunny air. Harriet asked if there were always the same animals on the summit. I told her I had seen Bighorn sheep tracks and mountain lion tracks there. Just once—when I was up with another little girl—I had seen a cottontail rabbit on the top, but I could not understand how he came to be there. Bluebirds, robins, ptarmigan, eagles, and weasels sometimes come to the summit.

We looked at the many-colored lichens upon the rocks and at the green leaves of the purple primrose and the stalks of the yellow avens. They were growing in little patches of sand between rock slabs. Harriet asked where the plants and the mountain top birds came from. I told her that a number of the same plants and animals were found in the far north around the Arctic Circle. At one time, many thousand years before, the Ice King had sent his glaciers a few thousand miles from the north, driving Arctic plants down on the moving ice and ptarmigan in front of it. These plants and birds had made their home on the mountain tops and remained after the ice melted away.

Harriet's aunt had told her that the Alps are much colder and snowier than the Rocky Mountains. No one lives as high in the Alps as the mountain valley where we were living; timberline—the forest edge—is at 6,500 feet there, and no plants or birds live above the altitude of 9,000 feet.

As we stood for a moment before beginning the descent Harriet turned and looked silently at the far-distant, magnificent views to the north, south, east, and west. Not a question was asked and I have often wondered what impression they made upon her.

After having a little more than an hour on the top of the Peak we started slowly homeward. When a little below the altitude of 12,000 feet we dismounted and searched among the boulders for the columbine. Luckily we found a beautiful specimen with its silver and blue petals waving on a slender stalk that stood several inches higher than Harriet's head. The columbine is the state flower of Colorado, having been selected by a majority vote of the school children, and is mentioned for our national flower.

Harriet looked again and again at the strange little trees at timberline and watched eagerly for the bears. We talked about the things we had seen. She asked many questions about the trips other climbers had made, and I told her of experiences on rainy days, on snowy days, and on wintry days. She was most interested in my moonlight climbs and wished she might some time go up at night.

Of the two hundred and fifty-odd trips which I made as a guide to the summit of this great old Peak, the trip with Harriet is the one I like best to recall; and I am sure, too, should Harriet live three score and ten years she will remember the day of her successful climb to the summit of Long's Peak.

This climb, as I remember, was in September, 1905. Some years later I heard that Harriet was graduated from a girls' college in Texas. I often wonder what has become of her.

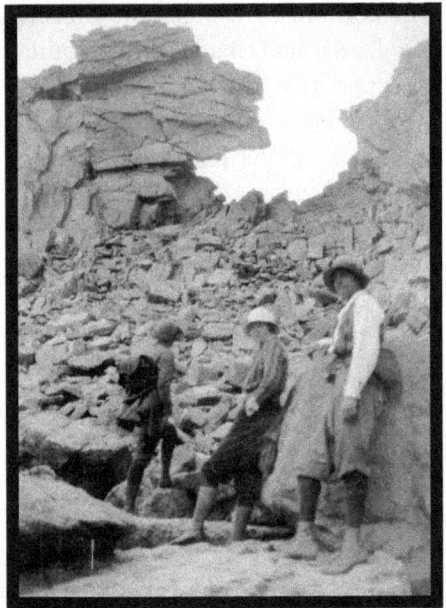

At right: Elizabeth Frayer Burnell (left), Harriet Peters (center), and Miss Brooks near Timberline on Long's Peak, July, 1928.

At left: Miss Brooks (left), Harriet Peters (center), and Elizabeth Frayer Burnell on top of Long's Peak.

Three years she grew in sun and shower,
When Nature said, "A lovelier flower
     On earth was never sown:
This child I to myself will take:
She will be mine, and I will make
     A lady of my own.

"Myself will to my darling be,
Both law and impulse; And with me
     The girl, in rock and plain,
In earth and heaven, in glade and bower,
Shall feel an overseeing power,
     To kindle or restrain.

"She shall be sportive as the fawn
That wild with glee across the lawn,
     Or up the mountain springs.
And hers shall be the breathing balm,
And hers the silence and the calm
     Of mute, insensate things.

"The floating clouds their state shall lend
To her: For her the willow bend;
     Nor shall she fail to see
Even in the motions of the storm
Grace that shall mould the maiden's form
     By silent sympathy.

"The stars of midnight shall be dear
To her: And she shall lend her ear
     In many a secret place
Where rivulets dance their wayward round,
And beauty born of murmuring sound
     Shall pass into her face."
                    —Wordsworth.

Long's Peak from Estes Park.

The Evolution of Nature Guiding

The primeval guide led his followers along the dim, wild life trail marked by hoof and claw. Primitive folk needed to find the way back to camp and to lead their associates to a discovered feast. Woodlore and the peculiar alertness which commonly goes with it made every Indian a born guide. The Indian took reckonings as he moved, and once over a route he knew its landmarks and its resources. Lewis and Clark in two emergencies were guided by Sacajawea, a sixteen-year-old Indian girl, who might be called a nature guide. Her mastery of the outdoors enabled her to lead the exploring party across the Rocky Mountains to places where she had not been before. Kit Carson and John Colter were excellent guides. Guides have encouraged people to go into new fields, among new scenes, to advance, to get somewhere.

MacMillan, in "Four Years in the White North," tells of a rare incident which illustrates the mastership of man over the obstacles of nature and the ability to use its resources. The thermometer was thirty-six below, and a blizzard had been roaring for hours when several sledge loads of Eskimos pulled up merrily in front of MacMillan's camp. The Eskimos were bound for two or three days' journey into the North, where they hoped to live off the country, and carried only a few pounds of food and a little oil upon their sledges. "They were real explorers," remarks MacMillan.

The nature guide finds treasures to right and left for his followers in territory which to most people appears barren.

The mention of a guide usually suggests an expert alpine or Canadian peak climber, a hunting guide in the North, the West, or Africa; an individual who can ride, shoot, cook a meal, pack a horse, and guide a hunting party to its goal.

Swiss guides are justly famous for their skill and their bravery on icy, storm-swept precipices and for their patience and endurance in overcoming the dangers and obstacles that beset the way of those who climb into the sky. Only a few people are physically fitted to follow the Swiss guide, and on the whole, peak climbing is a physical triumph. It is well worth while and is certain to continue. Nature guides offer natural history excursions more intellectual in their nature which may be enjoyed by almost everyone.

Natural history has been incidental to all previous types of guides, while to the nature guide it is the essential feature of every trip. The hunter's chief aim is to find and kill the bear, while that of the nature guide is to watch the ways of the bear and to enjoy him.

Some years ago in an editorial story in *Country Life in America* I called attention to our need of outdoor guides capable of arousing more interest in natural history. In 1916 I discussed the same idea, "Guides Wanted," in the *Saturday Evening Post*. The type of guide wanted is the nature guide. Nature guides are still needed but as yet there is no regular place for this training. While I have trained a few nature guides there appears to be a need for a State University or a Foundation regularly to develop nature guides.

It is probable that nature guiding will become a nationwide and distinct profession, and, though different, ranks with the occupations of authors and lecturers.

A nature guide is a naturalist who can guide others to the secrets of nature. Every plant and animal, every stream and stone, has a number of fascinating facts associated with it and about each

Jane Addams, wife of Alva Addams, a guest at Long's Peak Inn, explores with a guided group.

there are numberless stories. Beavers build houses, bears play, birds have a summer and a winter home thousands of miles apart, flowers have color and perfume—every species of life is fitted for a peculiar life zone. The why of these things, how all came about, are of interest. Touched by a nature guide the wilderness of the outdoors becomes a wonderland. Then, ever after, wherever one goes afield he enjoys the poetry of nature. This wonderland may be enjoyed around the world, forever. Wild birds sing, wild flowers bloom wherever streams ebb upon the sand or the seasons show their pictures.

Almost every locality has its old tree, its rare plant, its striking bit of geology. What natural history treasures are in the wild places of your locality? It would be a happy experience for any individual, either alone or with others, to make a nature survey of his locality with the idea of doing nature guiding or trail school work.

During each summer vacation a number of individuals are enriching their lives by getting intimately acquainted with the birds, animals, and trees of the locality visited. A nature guide in every locality who around his home or in the nearest park could show with fitting stories the wild places, birds, flowers, and animals, would add to the enjoyment of everyone who lives in the region or who visits it.

Before we realize it there will be municipal and private nature guides in every city park; official and private nature guides in state parks and in the national parks. Nature guiding is a splendid opportunity for young men and young women. It is a worthwhile life work and one that will add immeasurably to the general welfare of the nation.

We have been practicing, first alone then with assistance, the principles of nature guiding for some years in what is now the Rocky Mountain National Park. We hear that here are plans to use some form of nature guiding in both the Yosemite National Park and the Palisades Interstate Park.

The following slogans have grown out of our applications of nature guiding at Long's Peak, Colorado. They have interested many people and have helped extend the idea:

A child learns only when he is thinking, and nature's wonders compel him to think.

Every child asks questions. The nature guide answers questions intelligently and thereby brings forth other intelligent questions.

A nature room in every home containing photographs, nature books, and geological specimens. This would be a help in education.

Adventure for old and young—trail schools.

Trail schools always in session: day and night, summer and winter, rain and shine.

Trail schools train the senses. "The most important part of education has always been through the senses."—Dr. Charles Eliot.

Entertain your guests at home by a trip with a nature guide.

Boost for trail schools in every city park.

On top of Specimen Mountain, 1926.
Top: Sisters Elizabeth Frayer Burnell and Esther Burnell
Mills. Bottom: Esther Burnell Mills.

The few high class nature guides whom I have known had versatility and a background. They were not only masters of their own localities but had a good knowledge of the whole outdoors. They had camped and could tell others how to camp; had the resourcefulness to appreciate nature under all conditions—moonlight and starlight, in rain and snow—and could impart that pleasure to others; were masters of woodcraft—know how to build and to extinguish a campfire and how to select a camp site; understood horses and the packing of a pack horse. The ways and means of making their parties safe and comfortable, their knowledge of first aid, their vigilance in prevention of accidents, and their mastery of the trail, all became so much a matter of second nature that they were able to give all thought and energy to interesting their people in the natural history features. They had a quick eye for the interesting, the unusual, and the beautiful; they could use a camera.

The nature guide who understands human nature and possesses tact and ingenuity is able to hold divergent interests and scattering members of his party together. He appreciates, too, the eloquence of silence and is skillful in controlling, directing, and diverting the conversation of members of his party lest the beauty of the outdoors be marred by lack of discrimination of some one. He is master of the art of suggestion. He is a leader rather than a teacher. He has control of his party so that he may entertain, instruct, and command without their being aware that he is ruling with a hand of iron when the best results of the trip demand it.

Good outdoor books are a part of the nature guide's equipment and he is able to introduce others to good nature literature. And many of the eloquent nature lectures and much of the outdoor literature of the world may be in the nature of things be produced by nature guides.

It is not necessary for a guide to be a walking encyclopedia. He does not need to impose theories from printed authorities nor to consider nature books infallible; but a knowledge of the leading nature and scientific books should be a part of his equipment and may become a part of the enjoyment of those whom he interests. And, also, the nature guide should know Shakespeare and many of the great poems.

A nature guide is not a guide in the ordinary sense of the word, and is not a teacher. At all times, however, he has been rightfully associated with information and some form of education. Nature guiding, as we see it, is more inspirational than informational.

Vigilance in discouraging the picking of wild flowers is essential in any guide.

The nature guide arouses interest by dealing in big principles— not with detached and colorless information. He illustrates the principles of pollination, evolution, glaciation, migration of birds, mutual aid, and the fundamental forces of nature wherever he goes. He deals with the manners and customs of bird and animal life—the determining influences of their environment and their respondent tendencies—rather than with their classification. He creates more permanent interest in the biography of a single tree than in the naming of many trees.

Fortunate the individual who has nature for an outside interest. A well-known New York lawyer specializes during vacations on animal life—any animal—horse, chipmunk, or dog; this he watches and enjoys. It is well for each outdoor individual of limited time, while satisfying a general interest, to specialize on some one thing.

A guide also may specialize, but when he is out with a miscellaneous party he needs to be almost as universal as Nature herself.

In using the wondrous wealth of natural history the nature guide has extraordinary opportunities. He can be a mighty factor in helping people to determine how they will best spend their leisure hours. People are made and nations perpetuated through the right use of leisure time.

The following outline is a plan that we have used effectively in arousing interest in many an object. It may be adapted and used to fix interest upon any species of tree or plant, bird or animals; with modifications used in discussing geology. The idea of this plan is to give an interesting biography of every object considered—its name, classification, and family being wholly secondary.

Wind and water, birds and animals, scatter tree seeds —give them adventurous transportation in their search for a home. Most seeds are lost or destroyed. A few find an unoccupied place and

Enos A. Mills guiding a small group near Long's Peak Inn.

Starting out with sleeping bags to spend a night under the stars, guided by Elizabeth Frayer Burnell.

start to grow. Their place may be a favorable or unfavorable one.

A little tree peeps up into the big world and unfolds its leaves. It may be eaten by insects or by animals, burned by fire, trampled out, or uprooted. A number may be injured and still live on, and a few grow on uninjured.

Each year a tree puts on a thin coat of wood on the outside just beneath the bark. This coat grows over every twig and limb and the tree trunk. A tree grows higher by building at the top. A limb on the side that a small boy or girl can just reach will never be any farther from the earth. As the tree grows larger and larger it may be prayed upon by ants, borers, beetles, and woodlice, by gypsy moth and by caterpillars. But the chickadees, nuthatches, and other birds will eat the woodlice and the caterpillars, and Dr. Woodpecker will dig in after the borers and beetles.

Trees live from forty years to a few thousand years of age, and during their long life they stand in one place. They cannot travel, cannot run away from danger. In one place they face storm, wind, and drought. Every tree has an adventurous life. It is a home for the birds, it shelters plants, and gives shade and beauty to the world. It may bear fruit. It may become a flagpole or a ship mast and sail around the world.

Some trees like wet places, others dry places; some cold climates, others hot climates.

The pollination of trees, their evolutionary history, their geological records, ever are a delight.

Every flower that blooms, like every old tree, has an adventurous life, a brief and stirring biography. So, too, has every piece of red sandstone, and every great cobblestone in the lowlands. The red stone may once have been a piece of dark granite on top of the snowy peak. Or the cobblestone may have been torn from a cliff and shaped by a glacier that carried it for a thousand miles or more. Every handful of soil has a story stranger than any produced in fairyland.

The above plan can be adjusted and adapted to almost any subject under discussion.

To have made friends with one tree is better than to have learned the names of many trees. To have shared its experiences

169

through the seasons, to have watched the play of sunlight through the branches, the storms bursting over its head, the rain deepening the color of its bark—this is to feel the universal kinship of nature whether the tree be in a city park, is a lone tree, or one of a noble forest.

Realizing that people lose so much through their erroneous beliefs, I am trying so to feature the wilderness world that children will early adjust their lives to its splendid influences.

Altitude is helpful.

No American animal is ferocious.

Nature must be classed as friendly.

Wild animals and birds play frequently and with enthusiasm.

Nearly all species of birds and animals are endeared to home— that is, they live within the bounds of a local territory—and many have a permanent home.

Nothing equals the helpfulness of nature. But unfortunately the vast majority of people suppressed by busy and conventional conditions believe that outdoor excursions are uncomfortable and dangerous, that altitude is harmful, that most wild animals are ferocious, that nature, and especially the weather, is unfriendly; that animals are dull beasts led by instinct and are irresponsible, wandering gypsies; on the whole, it is believed that nature has nothing of value to encourage association with it. Nature guides can help in having nature appreciated at its true worth, in cultivating hospitality to changes of nature, and in welcoming all kinds of weather and each new experience.

Pioneer men and women have in all ages been famed for their alertness and individuality. They are keen and alive and they are happy to be living. Whitman makes the astounding assertion that all grand poems, all heroic deeds, were conceived in the open air. Certainly it is true that nature had something to do with the education and the inspiration of many of the great men and women who lived heroic lives, who did much to promote the glory of the growing world.

The magnificent influence of nature is revealed by many poets. Wordsworth eloquently pictures this in "Three Years She Grew"; William Cullin Bryant in "Thanatopsis"; and Shakespeare in many

170

lines, especially in the outburst of universal sympathy in King Lear's magnificent prayer on the storm-wild heath.

Although Australia and New Zealand were settled chiefly by convicts, these convicts under another sun and sky, with new opportunities and with the many-sided helpfulness of nature, quickly developed people as kind, alert, and unselfish as any upon the globe.

Mother Nature is ever ready to train the growing child. By using our wonderful national parks or other wild places we may give the boys and girls of today even better nature training than the pioneers received from their environment. Huxley says: "Knowledge gained at second hand from books or hearsay is infinitely inferior in quality to knowledge gained at first hand by direct observation and experience with nature."

The poetic interpretation of nature was a prominent factor in the education of Helen Keller. In "The Story of My Life," she says:

"For a long time I had no regular lessons. Even when I studied most earnestly it seemed more like play than work. Everything Miss Sullivan taught me she illustrated by a beautiful story or a poem...She introduced dry technicalities of science little by little, making every subject so real that I could not help remembering what she taught."

Darwin, who appears to be the most influential man of the last century, was anything but a book man. He met the requirements of school and college with difficulty and with reluctance. But field excursions aroused his powers and gave splendid purpose to his life.

Elizabeth Cady Stanton, as a little girl, was fascinated with running water, moonlight, and the mystery and sounds of the night. Often after the nurse had tucked her in she climbed out on the windowsill and sat listening and wondering for an hour or two.

As a boy Humboldt was kept out of school and encouraged to ramble in the wild, thus developing initiative and independence. Humboldt and Lincoln appeared to have been chiefly indebted to nature for their vision which they afterward helped realize for the world.

Froebel appreciated the value of natural history material for little children.

Charles G. Adams, perhaps the leading authority on ecology, has pointed out the significance of the response of animal and plant life to environment.

Recent museum groups embody the spirit of nature guiding—giving the manners and customs, the friends and enemies of wild life.

"The Nature Study Idea," by Liberty H. Bailey, is the most comprehensive and complete discussion concerning the helpfulness of nature that I have seen. His attitude is stated from a number of angles and he strongly commends the poetic interpretation of nature.

He says: "The subject (nature study) is not a formal part of the curriculum; and thereby it is not perfunctory. And herein lies much of its value—in the fact that it cannot be reduced to a system, is not cut and dried, and cannot become a part of rigid school methods...Whatever the method, the final result of nature teaching is the development of a keen personal interest in every natural object and phenomenon...Fundamentally, nature study is seeing what one looks at and drawing proper conclusions from what one sees...Nature study is not the teaching of facts for the sake of facts. It is not giving information merely...The artist and the poet know this world, and they do not know it by mere knowledge or by analysis. It appeals to them in moods, not in details."

We could hardly believe our senses except when hungry or while father was thrashing us.

When I was a boy in Scotland, I was fond of everything that was wild, and all my life I have been growing fonder and fonder of wild places and wild creatures.

Naturally inherited wildness in our blood ran free on its glorious course as invincible and unstopable as the stars.

Nature saw to it that besides school lessons and church lessons, some of her own lessons should be learned.

I was only leaving one university for another; the Wisconsin University for the university of the wilderness.

In drying plants, botanists often dry themselves. Dry words and dry facts will not fire hearts.

—John Muir.

The Development of a Woman Guide

A number of nature guides are women. Their number will increase. Their work is identical with that of men guides. In this chapter are glimpses of some of the field experiences and some of the driving forces of environment that resulted in producing one woman nature guide. The name of this woman is omitted at her request.

"She's the woman who made the fifteen-mile moon-light walk across the mountains in the snow," said one of the waiting group, as a young lady in knickerbockers, having adjusted the snowshoes strapped across her shoulders, left the post office.

"Oh," said another, "that was nothing compared with the thirty-mile trip which she made alone across the Range."

"Evidently she is a woman with a purpose in life," remarked the postmaster, looking out the window at the graceful figure swinging easily up the street. "She came out here from the East last fall determined to become a good mountaineer, and took up a homestead near MacGregor Pass. She knows college and business life and her own mind, and apparently she knows how to walk and enjoy it. Undoubtedly she'll make good in her ambitions to succeed out of doors."

Esther Burnell Mills and Enos A. Mills take a moment on the
steps of Long's Peak Inn.

Esther Burnell Mills
and her sister, Elizabeth
Frayer Burnell on the
trail.

This homesteader had seen twenty-seven summers and life had agreed with her. Her hair was red, and so too were her cheeks. She was five feet five, and weighed about one hundred and twenty. She had walked down to the village this November afternoon from her cabin four miles away, to get the week's accumulated mail and a few provisions. Darkness was already settling down over the pine-purpled mountains when she stopped to make a call. But she was not afraid of the dark—rather, she enjoyed night walks and walks in all weather.

"It is too late for you to think of going home tonight," said Mrs. Pond when her caller began adjusting her shoulder pack. "It will be dark before you can reach the canyon. Stay with us and go to Mrs. Samuel's card party."

"No," was the reply, "I must get home."

Then Mr. Pond came into offer hospitality and advice and to enter objections against her going. He remarked that bears had been recently seen near the canyon.

"Well, I'll certainly start at once," said the homesteader, smiling; "I have been wishing I might see a bear."

And off she started alone through the snow. And why had this young woman given up business to mountaineer?

A consulting decorator for a nationwide business firm and in love with her job, she overworked and eventually had a nervous breakdown. During the months of enforced rest she had had time to think, and did so. Many things in business life, she had decided, were wearing without seeming really necessary or worth while. Once in a routine of work, the average individual ceases to grow— ceases to be the architect of his own fate. She found herself wishing to get away from the city with its exacting demands, to a simple form of existence where money, people, and society were secondary. Then came the opportunity to homestead.

It was dark when she reached home from the village. After building a fire she sat down to read her letters. One was from the New York classmate whom she had invited to share her cabin and her mountain experiences. Her distressed artist friend, after thinking over the matter for a number of weeks, at last wrote:

"You are nearly as crazy—yes, I guess you are a little farther

Esther Burnell Mills.

gone than I am. Your letter thrilled me to death, I assure you, but being East in a comfortable, steam-heated home, two stories up, I can't help but wonder how it could be done, and we come out of it alive. I always did and always shall want to come West, but I must say I never quite worked myself up to thinking I could really enjoy living in the midst of the great unknown in a log cabin with one other person, and that person no stronger than myself, with no conveniences, and likely to be completely buried in snow at any minute.

"Now, if this hadn't been actually put before me as a proposition, my theorizing might picture it as the most wonderful experience I could wish for—yes, I should *love* to be snowed in and have wolves howl outside, and get the whole atmosphere thoroughly absorbed into my system, as you probably have done already...I wonder if you have sort of gone crazy about the place, the way those wanderers do who go into the mountains and never come back. If so, I think you need a guardian. You must have some strong person with you, and a dog, a big dog. Where is the nearest doctor? Facts are not pleasant things to rub into your dreams when you're dreaming, but they're mighty pleasant things when you're living."

The wild predictions of the city lady, who had no knowledge of the romance of homesteading, and was without sympathy for the simple, splendid life that may be lived in the mountain frontier, did not come true.

City people and others have listed several absolute necessities for every homesteader: a gun, a dog or a cat, a sewing machine, a victrola, a telephone, a burro, and, of course, a companion. This independent, individual homesteader possessed none of these so-called essentials, but she had a greater possession than they could have given her. She had "Happiness." In these lines you have a good glimpse of her life and of herself during her first winter of homesteading:

"Happiness"

My lot is a strangely happy one
Though far from the busy mart;
I live on my homestead all alone,
With ever a song in my heart.

And if perchance I tire of home
Away and away I go—
To gypsy by a stony brook,
Or campfire in the snow.

When wily wind blows fierce and strong,
Or cloud and mist allure,
I don my very oldest togs,
And picnic then for sure.

My thoughts are as free as the mountain air,
And never a care have I:
Where I live alone in a little hut
And not even the road goes by!

In this mountain frontier neighbors are separated by magnificent distances. Yet this young woman visited all her homestead neighbors, journeying from two to sixteen miles on foot. Last Christmas she and one of the other women homesteaders who lived 15 miles away walked to a midway place and had a merry campfire lunch among the pines. Alone she explored the forests and canyons. She climbed peaks, studied trees, and watched birds, beavers, mountain sheep, and other wild life. All alone, winter as well as summer, she made excursions, camping wherever night overtook her. Sometimes, too, she tramped by moonlight.

Many an evening in a wind-sheltered nook in the woods she cooked a scanty supper in the edge of a friendly campfire. After supper, if there was sufficient wood at hand for the night, she sat for a time watching the fire and thinking such thoughts as a lone, outdoor woman thinks. Often she wandered from the fire, better to have a look at the starry landmarks in the wide and trailless sky. After a few hours of perfect sleep in a sleeping bag she rose early and eagerly watched for the fires of sunrise from some commanding crag.

Her homestead consists of one hundred and twenty acres of mountain scenery, much of which is on edge. The land is covered with scattered growths of western yellow pine, Douglass spruce, and quaking aspen—the fairy aspen of which she has written so charmingly. A granite cliff towers several hundred feet above the house. From her front door you look westward up Fall River canyon, and beyond where the snowy peaks of the Continental Divide go far up into the sky. In front of the house is a garden of a few acres. Just outside her window is a table for birds. Chickadees and camp-birds were the only callers while I watched. Occasionally wild mountain sheep and deer confidingly follow an old game trail near the cabin.

The cabin in which she lived alone was called "Keewaydin," the Indian name for the Northwest or home wind. She drew the plans for it and helped to build it; designed her furniture and made a number of the pieces.

Anyone with a nose for news would have seen a story in the life of this young woman. When I called to get the story there was more reserve than I expected to find in an art school graduate.

"I understand that you helped shingle your house," I said, hoping to start her talking concerning building craft.

She smiled and answered: "Yes, the report was out that I shingled as fast as a man, and if it is still circulating it may be faster now!"

Knowing that friends had accused her of loafing—"of wasting her best years homesteading," I asked: "Have you read Stevenson's 'Apology for Idlers?'"

Instantly she flashed up, but with face melting into a smile, replied: "If you really have absorbed it and appreciate it, I'll say 'yes'." And then she added: "But it is not necessary to write a book, create a masterpiece, or evolve some labor-saving device for the recluse to feel justified in separating himself from the affairs of the world. If he values the power that lies in simple things and the height and breadth of vision that comes from a close contact with nature, that is sufficient. An overpowering desire to get away from the superficialities of life can only be satisfied by taking up that unfettered existence where truth is unvarnished and beauty is undefiled. No, it does not require courage to do what you want to do—to homestead, for instance—but it did take courage to say 'no' to the directing advice of relatives and intimate friends."

"And why homestead?" I asked, feeling that she fully appreciated the higher opportunities that go with homesteading.

"Our ancestors," she began, after a few minutes' thought, "who pioneered either through choice or necessity, labored that their children and their children's children might be 'better off' than themselves. But is it not for each of us to decide anew just what is 'better' for ourselves, and for those with whom and for whom we are living of the present and of the future? Does the 'better off' lie in vainly struggling to outdo our neighbors in accumulating possessions? Or will we find it by holding on to those fine, sturdy, fundamental qualities that make for strength of

179

body and happiness of spirit? The test of all effort should be not how much it gives us, but how deeply it makes us live."

Realizing that she had carefully considered all sides of the subject, I waited for her to continue. Her views of homesteading were convincing, as she disclosed them further:

"A homestead offers infinite opportunities for self-development and enjoyment. Here time is the willing slave rather than the compelling master; here a hobby may be ridden with a reckless abandon or with a prolonged exactitude impossible in the routine of city life. And, if your leaning is along the line of nature study, fortunate are you, indeed, if you have no other companions than those faithful allies of the brain—keen ears and eyes. Who is there who would not enjoy, for a time at least, the unbroken silences and all-enveloping solitude of a hermit's habitation? Who would not appreciate an opportunity to allow the mind and heart to travel together on limitless journeys into the past and future, gathering facts, creating fancies, that mould and shape new and bigger conceptions of life?"

The warm feelings of this woman, whom the world would regard as a self-exile, again and again reminded me of the words of the exile who wrote: "Life's more than breath and the quick round of blood." She is creative and courageous. Her refreshing enthusiasms are colored with high ideals. Of course she has definite ideas concerning education. She feels that schools are too much given to memorizing and to little to developing the powers of performance; that the senses are neglected; individuality and the creative faculty suppressed; and the wonderlight of imagination extinguished.

I was thinking that before long she might do something big, so universal were her sympathies, and I finally asked:

"You have become a good mountaineer, you also appreciate the facts and the poetry of natural history, why not become a translator of the great book of nature?"

"For years," she replied, "I have wished that others might have the strange delight from nature that I enjoy. And I have been trying to develop myself so that I might give its appeal to people."

"This can be done," I said, "you are fitted for a guiding

career."

The outings which she enjoyed usually were made alone and sometimes they were adventurous. The nearest settlement on the other side of the Continental Divide is thirty miles away. This is reached by trail—a trip across the summit, 12,500 feet above the sea, and then down through fifteen miles of rugged, forested mountains. She resolved to make this journey afoot and without a guide.

She had been on the summit midwinter, but this snowshoe trip was less eventful than her spring experience. It was a trip that few men had made alone, and local people had concluded that a woman could not make it if she tried. Her success literally startled the natives both sides of the Divide.

It was late spring and the winter accumulations of snow were soft, melting rapidly, and flooding water everywhere. Snowdrifts and soggy places full of flowers covered the steep and dangerously slippery slopes. But she reached the summit by noon. After eating a lunch on these heights, more than a thousand feet above the limits of tree growth, she started down the icy steeps into un-known wilds. She crossed the debris of recent land and snow slides. Everything was slippery, slipping, or ready to slide. But she came down to timberline without starting anything and without a slide herself.

Then for ten miles the trail led through deep snowdrifts and swollen streams. She crossed on doubtful logs; sometimes with the logs under water she hitched across astride the log in the roaring current. In places she waded to her knees. Just as darkness was settling down, all bedraggled, but enthusiastic, she arrived at the end of her journey. She took a longer, less perilous way returning —a two day trip that gave her new, though less rugged, scenes.

This outdoor woman had a purpose—a vision. Daily she accumulated experience and information. These she handled like an artist. She held on to the essentials only and made these enrich her life. Then, too, she had wide sympathies and in improving her opportunities to learn and grow it was with the idea of being able to serve others. She had steadily developed since the day she arrived. She had secured leisure and had used it.

Last summer she was a nature guide—an interpreter of nature—in the Rocky Mountain National Park, licensed by the Government. Old people gave her their attention, children were excitedly interested, and everyone was exercising and learning all at once. A trip with a nature guide is a rare influence for children. Eagerly they look and they listen; they see, they search, and they think. It is an alluring and most effective way of arousing the child mind so that it wants to know, so that it starts investigating and exploring, so that it insists on finding out.

This new occupation is likely to be far-reaching in its influences; it is inspirational and educational. Anyone who has a vacation or an outing in contact with nature will have from the great outdoors its higher values as well as a livelier enjoyment if accompanied by a nature guide.

Many of the visitors to national parks are nature enthusiasts, they appreciate having someone out with them who can interpret some of the wealth of local nature lore. There is geology, the story of the glacial landscapes, the ways of resident birds and the birds that come from southland for summer and to nest; beaver houses, Bighorn mountain sheep, brilliant Arctic flowers, the habits of trees, and the romance of everything.

Although everyone has inherited outdoor instincts which awaken with opportunity, yet, so long have most people been segregated from contact with the primeval—wild flowers, wild life, and crumbling, half-vine-concealed cliffs—that they welcome an intelligent and tactful interpreter of nature's ways. Such a guide enriches the outing, fills it with information, enjoyment, and vision.

A nature guide is doing the work of the world. Our homesteader had the art and the vision which enabled her to make these outings permanent, purposeful, growth-compelling experiences. They had none of the movie madness, nor the legend-diverting magic, but they gave a definite contact with the real world of life. Nature-guided excursions are educational and possess astounding possibilities for arousing the feelings and developing the unlimited resources of the mind.

No, this young woman was not wasting her time homesteading; it enriched her life, filled it with eagerness and delight. "To miss the joy is to miss all," says Stevenson in his immortal "Lantern Bearers." She is not missing it. The world may not know it, but she is as happy as Stevenson's boy with the precious hidden lantern on his belt. In the work of nature guiding she has found her place.

Publisher's note: The friend that Esther met was Katherine G. Garetson. For her version of the Christmas outing, please see *Homesteading Big Owl*.

William Neal and Esther Burnell Mills near Bluebird Lake, Wild Basin, Rocky Mountain National Park.

The Out-Of-Doors With A Nature Guide

Relaxation - Adventure - Education

Story of the Ice Age   Birds and Wild Life
Mountain Lakes   Trees and Flowers
Beaver Colonies   Timberline

"The woods are made for the hunters of dreams,
The streams for the fishers of song,
To those who hunt for the gunless game
The streams and woods belong"

Elizabeth F. Burnell, A. M.
(Univ. of Mich., Bryn Mawr.)
Nature Guide for Enos A. Mills
Long's Peak Inn, Longs Peak, Colorado

Authorized as a NATURE GUIDE in the Rocky Mountain National Park by the National Park Service.

Outdoor experience in Canada, the Bermudas, on Mobile Bay and at Spirit Lake, Iowa.

Available for special trips, summer or winter, day or night, in all weathers, for the Denver Mountain Parks, for the Pikes Peak region and elsewhere.

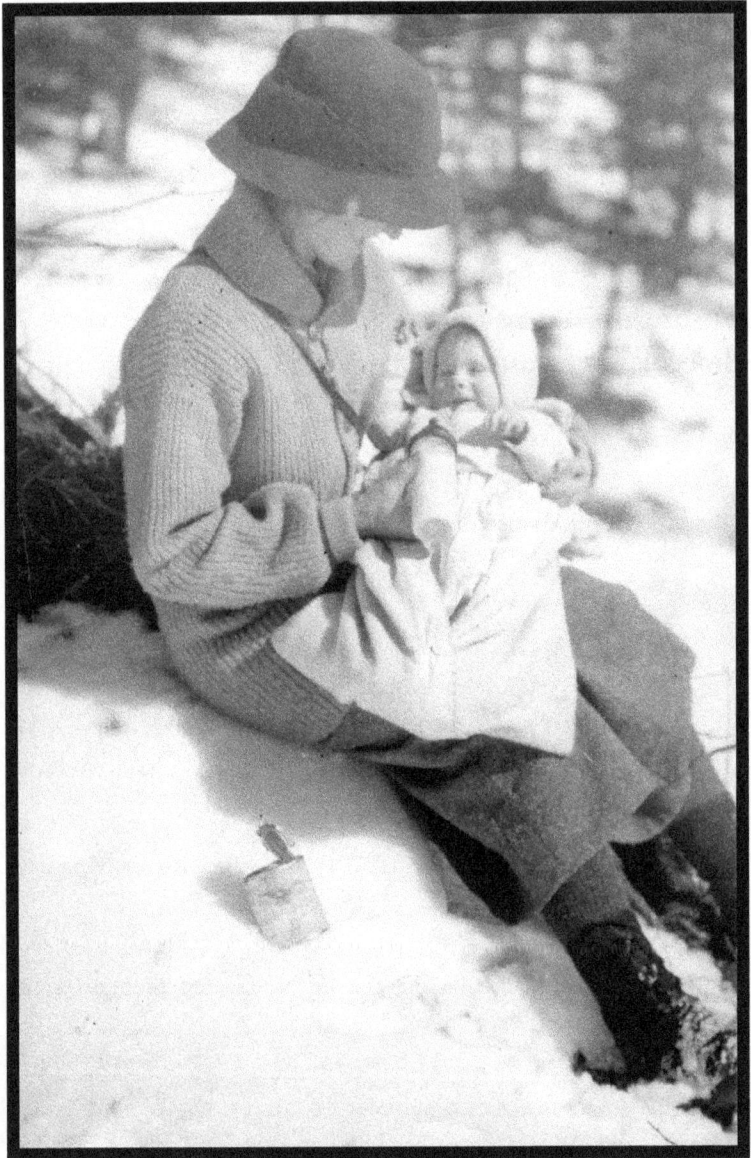

Esther feeds baby Enda on the trail.

To laugh often and much; to win the respect of intelligent people and the affection of children; to earn the appreciation of honest critics and endure the betrayal of false friends; to appreciate beauty, to find the best in others; to leave the world a bit better, whether by a healthy child, a garden patch or a redeemed social condition; to know even one life has breathed easier because you have lived. This is to have succeeded.

—Ralph Waldo Emerson

Enda

by
Esther Burnell Mills

Spring is a sly trickster up our way, slipping in an April sky, a burst of pussy willows or a Red-Wing's call, when the calendar registers only February or early March. Long before the lengthening days of sunshine have conquered winter's deepest snowdrifts, aspen buds have swollen to the point of bursting. All our mountain valley seems suddenly filled with a throbbing undercurrent of awakening life.

For into these scenes came baby Enda—the very spirit of spring itself! All energy, eagerness she was, springing into life like an early flower. A late April snowstorm greeted her but she came as undaunted as a bright anemone, and as well equipped as any native product for life in the mountains.

Enda's calm, sunny nature seemed to me a reflection of her father's. If the forming of a child's character is influenced during the first few days, certainly her father had all the credit. His big armchair, piled high with pillows, was her first bed. He was her first nurse, and his study was her temporary nursery. I am sure for the first thirty-six hours he didn't sleep a wink. Perhaps he was wondering if that bed was big enough to hold her. She was a lively five and a quarter pounds.

He accepted this new factor in his life so completely that even when a caller came one day that there was no thought of introduction. Enda decided to make herself known during a lull in the conversation, and her father answered the caller's astonished expression with "Oh, didn't you know we had a new nature guide?"

Summer, with its tourist population was upon us. No stranger was allowed to pick her up, and many would-be friends were turned away without even a look if she was sleeping. Her father knew that all young animals have to be allowed to wiggle, stretch and sleep, oblivious of the outside world. He knew that demands from the inside world make themselves known, promptly and specifically, if there were no other undue disturbances. He had raised, and of course fed, a family of orphaned bluebirds when still a boy himself, and later had adopted a pair of grizzly cubs and given them a good home.

The play of young animals has always been one of his most interesting pursuits, and he enjoyed Enda's babyhood from the psychological viewpoint that through play we reach our highest development. When I expressed surprise at his general adeptness with infants, he confided to me that during his first winter in Colorado, one of his special duties had been to take care of the baby Sunday evenings while the ranch family went to church. He intimated that the experience had been quite insightful into the world of the young.

Of all the young animals her father had acquainted himself with, Enda reminded him most of a grizzly cub. Her knowing grunts and quick responses to little attentions seemed to bespeak an intelligence which justified his complete study. He never came into the cabin, (which was several dozen times a day that summer), that he did not go directly to an observation point, if it was only a crack in the door. He liked to stalk upon her, to take her unaware. "I see you," he would have the unfair advantage of saying, when he discovered himself being watched.

Enda was his match. Even his rubber-heeled shoes on the porch were very early a signal for attention. Enda and her father understood each other perfectly. It seemed to be a theory shared in common, that babies sometimes need to see objects from an upright position. He conversed with her about these objects, as they walked around the room; the books in the shelves, the burning logs, the stones in the fireplace, the bark on the rustic table. He was constantly drawing her attention to the things around her, rather than to her own fingers, nose and toes. Enda responded in her own way—with rapt attention. Even this early there was a bond of companionship between them.

There was a strong personal resemblance between Enda and her father, which was often remarked upon. He was shyly amused at the comment of a sensible old lady, "She is a beautiful baby, and how she does resemble you!" Her profile certainly suggested his, so too did her blue eyes, which were alert and deep-thinking, and even her hair was soon discovered as being a sandy brown.

With all the wonderful opportunities for Enda's mental and physical development so obvious, to us at least, it was often amusing to hear the general solicitations regarding her future. "What will you do when it is time to send her to school?" was almost the first, and certainly the most frequent question. It seemed to be a matter of deep concern that a child should have to face the possibility of being brought up without any real "advantages." To be sure the nearest school was nine miles away. For six, eight or even ten years, what does a formal school matter, with an abundance of other influences to stimulate wholesome activity? The school's advantages are balanced with the disadvantages after all, of teaching *en masse* and of the learning method used by each child's mind. The importance of keeping up with a child's individual enthusiasms with personal attention, especially during the first six years when the mind makes its greatest development is enormous. Even if parents are not so situated as to supply the fullest possible background, personal involvement is beneficial. Their own education, no matter how "deficient" or how long suspended, is stimulated anew by the child's exuberance.

Enda was a continual stimulus. She knew our daily routine like a book, and was always a minute ahead of schedule. Even before she learned to talk there was an inquiring "Why?" in her eye that showed she was keeping tabs on the activities around her, and registered any variance in the usual scheme of things. She often welcomed the unusual with a relish, we soon realized it might call for a repeat performance.

This alertness and response to attention made her a ready

target for admiring friends. Many were the callers who gained a brief admittance on the grounds of having come "hundreds of miles" to see her! She had a smile for everyone and never missed an opportunity for making friends. Her bath hour was often a public reception, her airings an occasion for neighborhood gatherings. But it was always her father's step for which she listened, and she systematically woke up for his "goodnight" to her, at whatever hour he got his Long's Peak Inn guests to bed.

It was somewhat of a relief at the end of the summer to settle down in the peace and quiet of our own little cabin. Enda perhaps missed the frequent visitors, but she was to enjoy even more of her father's companionship. He was writing as usual that winter, among other things, a series of articles for *The American Boy Magazine*. In living over again the experiences of his boyhood in the mountains, what plans he must have been cherishing for Enda's camping and tramping, for watching and "waiting in the wilderness" with her.

Enda's kiddie-koop was in her father's workroom during all but her sleeping hours. She contented herself during the periods of "dictation" by the sound of his familiar voice, knowing that at the end of the story his undivided attention would be hers. His relaxation was her playtime too. Although naturally of a silent nature from having lived so much alone, his every move was now made a matter of conversation with Enda. "Do you think we better put some wood on the fire, Enda?" or, "Let's look up this number," as they ran down the pages of the telephone book together.

There were little surprises, too, that evoked Enda's imagination when she was least expecting it. From the next room her father would tip-tap on the wall to see if her ears registered properly. Having aroused her interest at this point, there was a sudden peek-a-boo from the door in the opposite direction. Her sense of smell was appealed to when a fresh can of coffee was opened. She soon developed the habit of smelling, before tasting, each new article of food that was added to her diet. The cutting of an apple in the room so stimulated her nostrils that she was early given a trial taste. After that, even the sight of an apple was exciting.

189

Enda inspects some pasque flowers with her teddy bear.

Fortunately, Enda was not over-burdened with toys. A red rubber sheep Baa-baa, and a Teddy-bear that came into her life that first summer, became inseparably a part of her existence. With one or the other she was perfectly happy. Her father made them a definite part of family life also, consulting them occasionally on vital points at issue. When things did not go smoothly, Teddy might be brought into the conversation and Enda left out of it— but not for long. This by-play was just too much for her sense of humor. "You're a joke," was an expression which her father often used to bring sunshine out of a storm.

A sense of humor is always a saving grace. Enda seemed to have this in good measure. Very frequently at a joke propounded by her father she would be the first to laugh, though the remark was not directly in the least to her, and probably she did not even understand it. But she recognized a joke! Perhaps she got the twinkle in his eye. Or does the voice take on a slightly different tone when the brain is stimulated to a novel expression of thought?

It never occurred to us to indulge in "baby talk" and apparently it was not necessary. I cannot but feel that her understanding of general conversation furnished her more to think about and enjoy than she would have had from the confusing foreign language supposed to be adapted to babies' ears.

Though Enda's social advantages were conservative that winter, she had the daily companionship of her father and mother to the fullest. On our walks and jaunts about the valley, Enda went with us. She watched our every activity with the greatest interest, knowing that she would at least be a silent observer, absorbing in all the events of the day.

Winter in the mountains is not all snow, wind and storm. Almost every day has an abundance of sunshine, and there are many warm, calm days mid-winter that encourage outdoor adventure. The best days were always taken advantage of, for our time was our own, and work was frequently suspended for a five or six mile walk to the beaver ponds or to trail the coyotes heard the night before.

Bundling Enda up in the good old-fashioned way did not allow the desired physical freedom, on her part or ours. A pack-sack was devised in which she was well supported and yet had perfect freedom. From the age of nine months she traveled this way with us. At the first evidence of either of us going out, she would make an effort to get up in her kiddie-koop, pointing excitedly at the pack-sack hanging on the door.

If the thermos bottle was prepared she was even more jubilant over the prospects, for she soon came to know this meant a longer walk than usual. Her father accepted this enthusiasm as fitting and natural in a "future nature guide," but it was quite evident to me that his own enthusiasms, intense at all times, were kindled anew in the fresh view-point which Enda gave to our outdoor adventures.

Her face beamed with happiness on these walks. She liked the easy swaying motion, and when a halt was made the "horse" was likely to receive a kick in the back from restive little feet. Her spontaneous response to each new interest which excited us was a continual surprise and joy. Sometimes she was fast asleep when we reached home, and great was her disappointment that the walk ended so soon.

Riding in a pack gave Enda many points of vantage. She was up in our world, her eyes on a level with ours. There was little that she missed. If one thing impressed itself more forcibly upon her attention than another, there was no indication of it. Her mind was busy building up impressions, forming a background for the activities which were to come later.

There was no effort made during this first year at formula teaching. She was quite busy learning from her surroundings. It was enough for us that Enda's babyhood should be merely a receptive attitude toward life.

Enda must have early begun to familiarize herself with the purely physical features of the landscape. The jagged skyline of rocks, pines and few lasting snow-piles must have gradually shaped itself into the form of seven prominent peaks whose names came to mean so much more to her later. The more striking aspects were doubtless often brought to her attention. Moonrise and sunset were ever of interest and commented upon, and even the blue, blue sky impressed itself on baby eyes.

We were not oppressed by the isolation, nor was Enda. In her little pack-sack she climbed mountains, explored beaver dams, skated icy ponds and became intimate with the sounds, colors and smells of wind, water and waving pines. She laid the cornerstone during her first year for the fullest enjoyment of life, by a friendship of the world around her.

Enda's interest in the pack-sack suddenly waned. At thirteen months she was clinging to the furniture and to daddy's knees. She was frequently warned, "watch your step," and "don't let the floor jump up and bump you." In case of doubt or speeding she always chose a sitting position.

It was very evident that Enda's whole thought was concentrated on getting out into that glorious June world. With the most appealing expression and pleading gestures, she would lead us to the door, pointing excitedly to all the interests that lay beyond. She was leading her father around by one finger at fourteen months, and the path between our cabin and the Inn was soon well-worn with little footprints. With lightning-like motions she kept up with his easy, springing steps. Off the beaten path she was usually swung under her father's arm, and from this position enjoyed making the daily rounds of directing carpenters, plumbers and house cleaners.

"Go walk," filled the horizon of her day. She made opportunity of the various comings and goings of our visitors to carry out her intensity of purpose. Seizing upon any finger available, she all too frequently attempted to speed and accompany the departing guest.

Just being out was not enough. At any suggestion of lingering near the cabin, she would pleadingly point away and beyond. She wanted to explore in every direction. The months of traveling in the pack-sack had unlocked worlds of interest to follow up. Marvelous changes had followed winter and she must have been impressed by the brightness of the new aspen leaves overhead, and the brilliant carpet of flower-land reaching out as far as she could see.

The noisy bees down in her own world, but ever just ahead of her, were among the early mysteries. Untiringly she trudged in chase, hoping to get a closer acquaintance with this illusive fellow. Bee was an important factor in her very active life this summer, for she lived among the flowers and he was ever luring her farther afield.

"Bee" was among the first, and certainly the most overworked word in her vocabulary at this age. It came to be used consistently and insistently as a synonym for "go walk." Any abridgement in linguistic expression she welcomed, but there were no shortcuts to pedestrian attainments.

Enda's sense of balance was perhaps a naturally inherited quality, or perhaps her physical center of gravity, or it may have

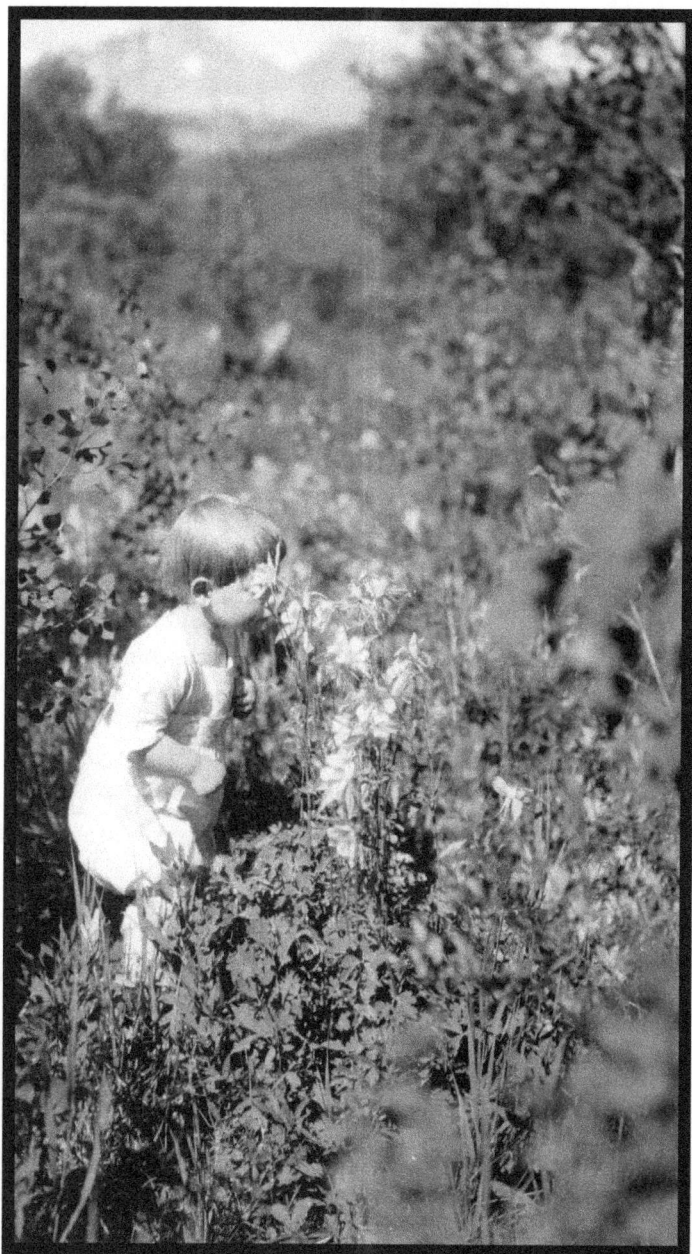

Enda smells the columbines.

been developed by her environment. Our grounds are sloping, the trails more or less rough with stones, the grass tall and unmown. After she was able to go unassisted, strangers were often alarmed at her speeding. Over sticks and stones that would have caused many an older child to stumble, she went without hesitation. Before the summer had passed, she could easily outrun any of us, except her father. Here again his training of grizzly cubs had served him to good purpose, for bears rate high in the world's long distance runners!

An unfortunate experience with an ant, unknowingly sat upon, brought this word forcibly into her vocabulary. She had felt, but not seen him definitely. Any unknown insect subsequently brought out the instant interrogation, "Ahnt?" When assured that it was not the insect of her previous experience, she proceeded to make its acquaintance with unbounded enthusiasm. She never went around stirring up ant hills, and there were many of enormous proportions which she might have investigated. At the merest suggestion of "Ahnt" she restrained her natural curiosity.

It is impossible to record concretely a child's mental processes, although watching all the tangible signs of growth and development. We were constantly amazed at the strides Enda made towards understanding from week to week. We could not judge the mental gymnastics behind the scenes, of the practice jumps she was making by herself, within herself. When the occasion for full-fledged demonstration arrived, then we were in awe! Her unconsciousness in achievement was perhaps the most interesting factor in her development. She was progressing through her own initiative. At any rate, there was no goal set, no applause awarded her, for we wished her to enjoy the purest spontaneity. And she did!

I started keeping a record of her development in understanding, of her reaction to life around her, near the time she was about a year and a half old. This had been suggested previously by her father but instigated by Enda. The incident which actually started this record was one which indicated her quick grasp of learning to sight objects.

The rabbits that play around our yard in winter and summer

always select a shady spot for their halts between dashes. Enda didn't notice that we had startled a rabbit in rounding a corner of the cabin. He stopped in the shade as usual. Telling Enda to look for him, I stooped and pointed to him with my arm on a level with her eye. I really expected her to concentrate her gaze on the end of my finger. But no. She came up behind me, sighted along my arm to the spot where the rabbit was sitting. I watched her eyes to discover if she really saw him. She kept her fixed gaze on the spot to which I was pointing, but not until the rabbit moved slightly did her expression change.

Enda had lived out-of-doors, come close to Nature in every waking moment through the summer. Even the little brook that rippled under her window must have been a happy accompaniment to her sleep. In the rain we had our walks, Enda high and dry in the pack-sack, and an umbrella over our heads. She loved this most of all; the raindrops pattering on the umbrella, dripping off the pine needles, running down the pine trunks, and making muddy puddles to splash through. Coming home after the shower had its thrill; the raindrops sparkling in the sunshine, the birds singing again, and the freshness of the forest in the dampness.

In the lull that came after summer, when the flower meadows were sleeping and the aspen leaves had fallen in all their glory, she must have been waiting for the next demonstration. It came with the first snow.

Running again and again to the window with excited exclamation of "Oh, my, oh, my..." she could hardly wait to be dressed and out in it. This new interested filled the day with activity. If she remembered anything of snow from the previous winter, it was not with this joy of tramping it under foot. Catching the softly falling flakes, only to have them vanish before her eyes, was exciting and mystical to her.

Then, what wonderful tracks we made! She looked at hers, then at ours. I had thought in the summer that her pleasure in the flowers had attained the capacity of her enjoyment. Snow seemed to be a rival, or at least a substitute and just as good! We must have walked miles that day without knowing it, for the changed landscape excited her to go to each favorite place to see it in new snow dress. The trees were strange and phantastic, fences and stumps were all beautifully decorated. But where were the mountains?! She pointed here and there, pondering wonders, if we were in a different world, or if someone had let down a curtain.

The brook absorbed her longest. The stream was not yet frozen. Watching the snowflakes melt away in the running water held a fascination even greater than she had known from throwing sticks and stones into its smooth surface. The first snow went in a few days, but the next snowfall and the next, each came as a new surprise and wonder. Always there were tracks and more tracks. Perhaps the greatest appeal was to the imagination. Where did the snow come from, and where did it go? must have been among the numerous questions forming in her mind long before actually put into words.

I was alone with Enda much of her second winter. Her father was away on a distant lecture trip, and I suppose no one can estimate her lonesomeness. Even our walks seemed to lose their intense interest.

She associated her father's absence with the telephone, for she had last heard his voice over long-distance from Denver. For weeks, each time the phone rang, she made a rush to answer it, thinking surely that he must be at the other end on every call.

One of her occupations was arranging the *pas partouted* mounts of our pressed flowers collection. They were most often taken upon the floor and displayed in rows against the wall. There was genuine distress when other operations in the household routine required their removal. At such times, I had to allow her time...she wanted to put them away herself, in systematic order on the shelf. Each was looked at thoughtfully, as though making some individual kinship. She recognized their unnatural, glass-imprisoned faces as her flower friends of the summer. I talked about them by name and recalled where we had seen them growing. They continued through the winter to hold more sustained interest than any of her large assortment of picture books.

The story that made the strongest appeal was a simple little book, by the title *"Timmy Tiptoes,"* in much the same style as Peter

Rabbit, and by the same author, the text held unending interest. Mr. and Mrs. Timmy Tiptoes lived an active and adventurous life, and lived it evidently in Enda's very own woods! The account of their nut gathering, their disagreements with the chipmunks and birds, and the appearance of a bear in the scene, was graphic enough to call for several readings at one sitting. All squirrels were henceforth known as "Timmy," and they were well known to Enda even at this time, though not as numerous in our midst as the rabbits. We frequently saw them and more frequently heard their chatter, upon our walks through the grove, and their storehouses of cones may have given added significance to their existence. It was not unusual to have a squirrel come to our bird table in winter, and it was evident from Enda's interest in "Timmy Tiptoes" that this noisy, active fellow had made a very definite impression on her.

We had one big experience this winter, Enda's first in coming close to big wild life. Stepping out on the side porch one snowy afternoon, we abruptly stopped a mountain sheep that had been leisurely approaching the cabin. It stood at attention for four or five minutes at a distance of fifty yards. The Bighorn was as much surprised as we. At our first move off the porch toward it, the sheep turned abruptly and beat a rapid retreat. The next day we went out and followed its tracks. It had entered the yard over a packed snowdrift that had blown against and completely covered the fence at one point. The tracks led up the Long's Peak Trail, but the ground was only partly covered with snow and we lost its footprints in the hard, bare gravel. Enda, however, was loathe to give up pursuit.

She frequently pointed out tracks in the snow after this, now having an interesting reference of cause and effect, they took on a new and deeper interest. She always wanted to follow them, and we often did. She had many examples that rabbits, squirrels, coyotes, deer, and even skunk lived and traveled the same trails that we did.

Enda early manifested two distinct sides to her nature, which we all have in a greater or lesser degree. One is the appeal of the purely imaginative, an enjoyment of the phenomena of nature

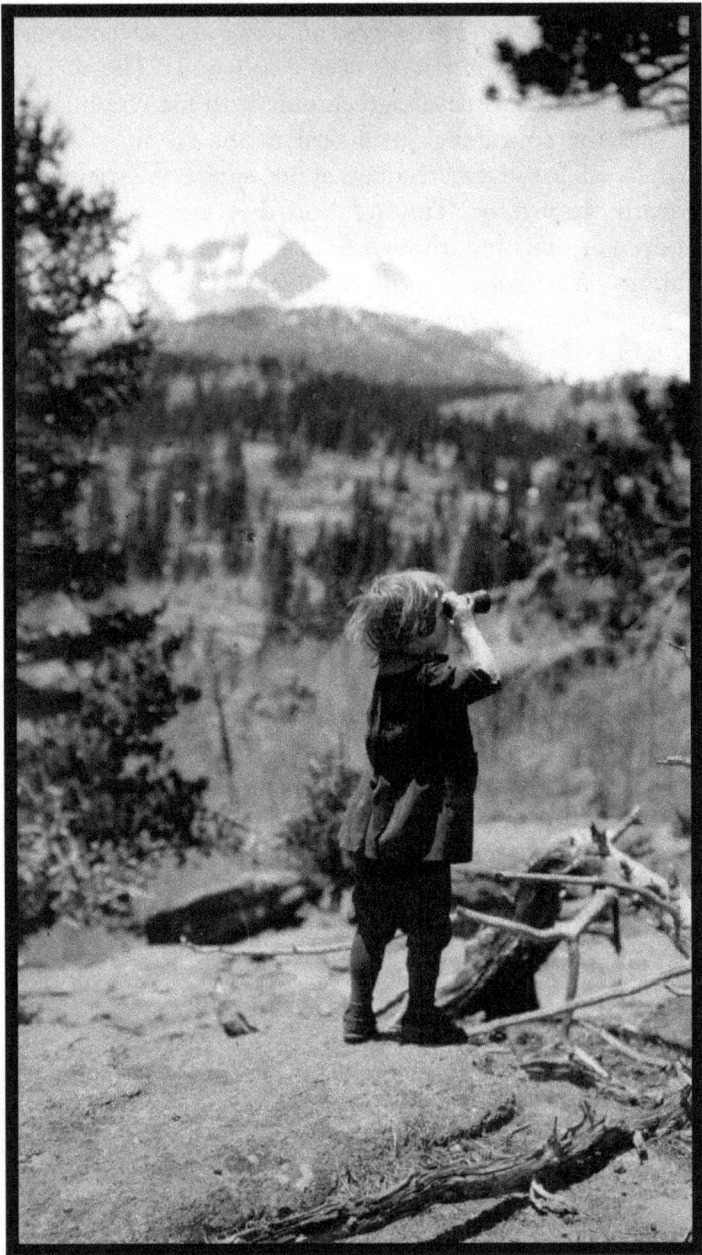

Enda looks through binoculars near Long's Peak Inn.

beyond complete comprehension; and the other is mastering the realistic side of life, the things within our control. Harmonizing all these influences cannot be overlooked in studying a child's development, for by keeping a proper balance is a rational outlook on life eventfully formed. A child's mind is grounded in reality, and when we give them anything less it confuses them.

Enda was at her best when out of doors, she was getting her greatest enjoyment when all her senses were being appealed to through her powers of observation and experience.

Enda's happiness knew no bounds when her father returned at the end of winter! She delighted in rushing to open the door, in bringing his arctics and helping him put them on, or anticipating various little services that her observation taught her most likely to produce smiles and hugs. She followed his every move and showed even a stronger inclination than formerly not to let him out of her sight! Sometimes he would express his next move in code to me, when an errand at the Inn made taking Enda inadvisable. Soon Enda learned all the codes; probably the word "Inn" was her best clue! She knew when her father's pencil stopped, something else was likely to be started; and she was always on the job, ready to start without notice.

Enda had not forgotten our sheep caller of several weeks earlier, and led her father out to the porch with excited gesticulations. Of course I had to be called upon to narrate the incident. The frequency with which she insisted her father should go to this porch, which was not our usual means of entrance or exit from the cabin, seemed to indicate that she was expecting that sheep to come again, and she wanted her father to see it.

Even along the dusty road she found tracks, for snow is not a permanent winter mantle in our valley. Always a good observer, one day she surprised us by exclaiming "Ged-dup, ged-dup." We looked around in every direction but there were no horses in sight. Then we noticed that Enda was pointing to the ground. We could not remember having called her attention to horseshoe prints, they probably held much more significance to her than to us.

She was determined not to talk, though I had made every effort to encourage conversation during our months alone, sometimes going as far as pretending not to understand what she wanted. The few words she used to express herself she used effectively.

It was evident that she had a good knowledge of the English language, though she did not use it, for she followed every remark with understanding. It was often amusing to see her shake her head when we used a sentence with "don't", "won't" or a negative of any kind. She agreed with us perfectly. When her father remarked for his own amusement of course, "You have a queer pair of parents," out came a very emphatic "umphah" (no), from Enda and a decided shaking of her head.

She was at all times a good "orderly," standing in readiness to return broom, dustpan, overshoes or mailbag to the proper place after use. This sense of order was frequently commented upon by others. It indicated also keen observation, that every incident in her life registered clearly and definitely. It was sometimes rather strenuous for the rest of us, and later gained for her the name of "the little executive." We could not help but speculate how Congress would be influenced under Enda's bright-eyed awareness keeping them on their toes!

Enda's constant reactions to most of the minor incidents of the day impressed me with the pure logic of her reasoning powers. The child's mind, if given accurate information to work upon, seems to be uniformly constructive. When at times destructive the mind is making an effort to discover the cause behind the effect. Even when most unreasonable, the child is usually trying to make the impossible, possible; to change the seemingly changeable.

Hurrying across the field after her father, when twenty-two months old, she stumbled and fell. Half rising, she looked back to see what had caught her foot; then getting up she stood and looked back again, and finally, though in a hurry to catch up with her father, she went back to the spot to see what had caused her to stumble. There were many small animal holes half hidden in the dried grass. She then picked her way more carefully, and joining her father, took his hand that she might hurry with safety. Usually she objected to being given a hand, no matter how much she had missed him!

201

It is only natural that we found daily enjoyment in watching the progress of our child's development, seeing the manifestations of her alert, busy mind. We realized that we were being closely watched too.

On a February walk I was surprised to see the stonecrop making a showing of new green leaves. I stopped and picked a leaf, wholly unobserved I thought, by Enda wandering on ahead. As we went on together she seemed to be looking for something. The next stonecrop in evidence caused her to stop and pick a piece, which she handed to me. There were other plants starting which she might have picked, she evidently thought I was particularly interested in this one.

Observing me trying to take a knot out of a string, Enda brought me a pin and insisted that I use it, as I had done on a previous occasion. Later she observed in silence for a few moments my efforts in trying to wedge a stone loose from the frozen ground, then brought me a stick to pry it up, without explaining the purpose of it. She recalled this from past experience, from a few weeks earlier.

Enda had her own little ways of side-play, doing the unexpected for her father's particular enjoyment. His usual comment was simply, "I see you." One day when we were out, Enda ahead as usual, I cautioned her with, "Go quietly, there is a rabbit." She had already seen him. Pointing in that direction, she remarked matter-of-factly to him, "I see you," and went on her way.

Imitation seems to be the strongest natural instinct perhaps for self-preservation. At our house this was given full play. If her father was writing, she was given a pencil and paper; if reading, she had a book to look at. Unfortunately these materials did not offer the absorption for her that they did for us. After a short time she would return them with an expression of, "I'm ready for something else."

When it came time for complete relaxation for everyone, Daddy would suddenly appear from no-where on all fours. Under tables, behind big chairs, out one door and in another, this mysterious animal was pursued; and sometimes there was a lively procession of animals, for not only did Enda quickly fall into the spirit of the game, but she insisted that mother join too. There was no scare allowed, for the bears at our house did not eat children nor behave unseemly. A merry romp and an appeal to the imagination were the only liberties allowed them. Sometimes Enda started this play by getting down on all fours and patting the floor to charm her father to join her. She liked to ride on his back, and often the bear was instantly transformed into a "Ged-dup."

Enda and Enos had many happy playtimes, and part of each day was devoted to being out with her. He never lost an opportunity for enchanting her imagination. Passing a glass door that the carpenters placed standing against the side of the building, he called Enda's attention to her reflection, then to the reflection of her doll. Having awakened interest in the little girl behind the door, he peeked behind it, saying "Where's Enda, I don't see her anywhere?" She appreciated this acting so much that repeat performances were called for, often reversing the parts of respective actors.

The early spring flowers had an influence on Enda, like beloved friends returning. They gave her something to look for and to think about—an outside interest that she enamored at this age. Though our life was too busy and varied to allow her to become the centre of interest, nevertheless she found many creative and constant ways of demanding our attention. Upon the flowers she lavished real affection of her own, with no other incentive than the unconscious response which they awakened in her imagination.

Enda was much concerned for the welfare of her little flower friends when a heavy April snowfall kept them blanketed for nearly three weeks. She enjoyed that snow with all her unbounded energy. She was more its match now than she had been in the early winter, and the warm, sunny days found her out with mica snowglasses and no complaining about sweaters, leggings and mittens. She all too often disapproved of being bundled up and could never understand the extra clothing that mother provided for outdoor activities. She was like her father in this, for he seldom added a coat or hat to his outdoor apparel, even in winter.

The paths shoveled through three feet of snow, soon left a trail of bare ground that Enda could follow in various directions. The snow banks nearly as high as she, were a further attraction. All the doll and animal tribe were carried out two by two to explore these miniature snow mountains. Shovel and pail were brought into play, and no child at the seashore ever had so much fun than she in her ocean of snow. It lasted interminably to us, so late in the spring, but for Enda it furnished endless occupation. A heavy rain finally carried the last of it away. All this undue moisture sent the chipmunks scurrying from their underground homes earlier than usual.

The constantly changing program of events kept Enda alert to make the most of every form of amusement which her environment of nature furnished. Her whole body was in sympathy with her eagerness of thought; whether it was speed in running, strength in holding her own against obstacles to be overcome, or in meeting emergencies that called for definite action. There was every form of expression in her movements; gentleness with the flowers, but vigorous muscular activity in throwing stones or leaping fallen logs.

At two her chief characteristics were intense enthusiasm for any interest at hand, perseverance in what she wanted to do, and an insistent determination "to help." She could not be persuaded from anything we did that was too hard for her; bringing in wood, sweeping with her own little broom, and even finding a pail her own size to carry water. Water in any form had a never-ending attraction, and scrubbing day was always hailed with delight. Hours were spent "pinkling," watering the flowers, after everything inside the house washable had received its quota of water.

Whenever possible, sometimes when it seemed almost impossible, we allowed Enda to carry out her eager suggestion of "do it my own self." It took longer of course, to accomplish the desired end. The confidence in herself gained through each hard-earned experience, doubtless opened up numerous avenues of interest, occupation and confidence which otherwise might have been forever closed.

Children are young animals and have an innate attraction

toward any active animal. How Enda chased the chipmunks and rabbits that played around her cabin! They were no more wild than she, and readily responded to attentions. Her father spent many patient hours showing her by example and explaining his tactics of calmness and deliberation, that "watchful waiting" is the charm that wins the confidence of animals.

Even so Enda could not resist rushing to meet them half way. Her nature was too active to be calmed down by words alone. When out by herself, however, she caught the spirit of the chipmunks' caution.

A game which we often played brought quick response from Enda. One of us would shut our eyes and stand still, while the others moved off a short distance and called. The "blind man" had to point in the direction and name the caller. Enda especially enjoyed taking the part of the blind man. Of course she did not always get the location exactly, but nothing was made of failure, for a sense of honor in not peeking was established, not in the results of the contest.

While watching a bluebird on a telephone wire nearby, and commenting on its having come to live near us, there was a sudden call from a blackbird. Wondering if Enda would confuse the two, I asked, "did you hear that?" She turned and pointed off in the direction of the blackbird's call, then resumed her interest in the bluebird.

She was noticeably impressed by the bird life around us. We encouraged them by keeping a bird table supplied in winter that was "safe" from predators. She was quick to discover that new birds came to nest near the cabin in springtime, and the bird songs that came so mysteriously from the treetops often caused her to pause and listen, whether they were in sight or not.

A young Downy Woodpecker was found just out of the nest one June day. Enos placed it on Enda's arm with rapt admiration and they had their picture taken and baby was returned to the nest. For days she tried to tell everyone about this rare experience. Her vocabulary was as yet very limited, but she would repeatedly recall the incident by pointing to her arm with exclamations of "baby bird," until we were compelled to interrupt the conversation of the moment to tell the story again.

A family of young bluebirds that left their nest on the corner of our cabin alighted within the enclosure of her yard on their first trial of wings. This gave Enda another excellent opportunity to get close to bird life. One of the youngsters was held by her father for her close inspection. She then rushed into the house for graham crackers to feed the young bird—her own favorite article of food. All day as the bird family lingered near, Enda devoted herself to watching them and trying to tempt them with small pieces of graham cracker which she resigned to eating herself.

Out of her personal contacts came may interests and questions. What kind of food *do* birds like? Where do they go in the winter? Where do they go at night? What kind of bird built this nest? Now the bird nests that were discovered on every walk meant more to her and out of the train of thought started by them, came an unlimited and natural interest in the kinds of homes that different animals had.

One of the magazines opened one day had an illustrated cover that aroused an excited series of "bow-wow-wows" from Enda. Her father was absorbed and did not notice her exclamations. As Enda continued her examination of the picture, her bow-wows became less and less positive, and finally ended with a rising inflection. Her father's attention being drawn to the picture, Enda's question "Bow-wow?" was answered with "No, coon." She repeated the name, a new one, and continued to look upon the animal with intense concentration. She never forgot the Coon's distinctive markings, and was always glad to meet him again in her animal books.

Realizing Enda's desire to experience life in all its forms and realities, we sought out ways and means of allowing her initiative full play. We purposely led her through the densest aspen thickets, where there were springy limbs to dodge; over logs and ditches and under fences, oblivious of the easier way round. Imitation would have followed any examples of reckless adventure, and we crossed the brook in the narrow places that she could jump, or on convenient stepping stones that she could navigate alone.

She early manifested a strong dislike for being helped. Allowing her to try things out developed a rather unusual sense of caution and a certain mastery of her own environment. The only time she unintentionally went into the brook happened when her running leap was intercepted by the admonitions of a visitor.

Fear was never suggested in any form, or a sense of terror substituted for correct understanding. Investigations in every direction were encouraged for her mental development and we felt it important for Enda to know the "why" of things. Of course knives and matches were carefully guarded, we had become acutely aware to use them with the utmost respect in her presence. Even these had to be tried out by Enda before our judgement was considered accurate.

There was never any request made to be carried home, even after long expeditions that must have made her leg-weary indeed. Up steep trails she insisted on trudging along alone, usually in the lead, the better to avoid a helping hand! She went out of her way to climb over rocks and logs, even though we stayed in the narrow and well-defined, if not straight path.

Enda's third summer was consumed with walking. The interest never lagged, and her little legs kept up with the interest. There was much more than mere physical pleasure in this activity. All her senses were alert; she was seeing, feeling, inhaling nature with every fiber of her being. A keenness of appreciation was made evident in many ways; by a look, a gesture, and in the unbounded energy with which she met every situation.

This ready response to life was a constant inspiration to her father. It was in a way I think, a satisfaction to him that she did not talk. He expressed himself in a few words, but always to the point. On our walks we talked but little, we had more opportunity for seeing and thinking when conversation took minor place. Anything unusual was the subject of comment, but for the most part we reserved our outings for the natural stimulus to mind and body that comes with complete relaxation. Enda seemed to feel something of the "subtle influences of nature," or perhaps she only acquired a similar attitude of receptiveness, for she was ever reaching up into our world of thinking and feeling.

We generally played "follow the leader" in our wanderings, but on the road Enda thought walking three abreast "the most fun." Holding to a strong finger on either side, she often took advantage of this order of march. Breaking into a run, which we must keep up with because of that firm grasp, at the opportune moment she would give a high swing that carried her forward mid-air until the restraints of her side partners slowed her down.

These little surprises, this spirit of play, was a pleasure to see. Her father was on the alert for giving surprises, too. Hide-and-seek in the grove was often sprung without warning. He just disappeared behind some big pine or rock and Enda immediately took her cue. We all had to hide by turns, though of course she took greatest delight when she was the one being sought. If we took too long to find her, she encouraged us by a quiet "hoo-hoo-ing," but usually the game was played in silence.

We all loved this pine grove within a few minutes walk of our cabin, and even on the busiest days we found time to make a visit. In winter sunshine or moonlight the dark shadows made wonderful tracery on the snow. Around the forest's edge came some of the first flowers of spring. Enda knew all the grove's resources—pine cones to gather for the fireplace, stumps to mount or leap, rock piles with beautiful mosses and lichens, mushrooms and spruce gum, and winter or summer, we were pretty sure to see "Timmy" or evidence that he had been about. He had one favorite place for hoarding his winter supply of pine nuts, and, judging from the enormous accumulation of pine scales, this place had been used by his ancestors as storage room and dining table for many generations. Enda loved to fill her hands with the soft, crumbly scales from this big pile of depleted cones. Throwing a handful into the air, as she had seen her father do, she thoughtfully watched the seedless "wings" float slowly, lightly down, after the heavier scales had fallen.

Owls often hooted from this grove at nightfall, and occasionally we were reminded by fragments of feathers and fur, that they had feasted on some of their neighbors. Coyote tracks were often seen too, and Enda was constantly looking for the fellow himself.

There was an interesting succession of tree growth in this bit of primeval forest. A giant yellow pine, several hundred years old, still showed scars from the fire of 1781. An even growth of slender Lodgepole pine had succeeded this fire and taken advantage of the clearing made by it. Numerous small spruce had more recently gotten a start in the protecting shade of the pine. A few limber pine claimed the most rocky places or the outer sunny edges of the grove. Enda imitated us when embracing these trees' "tummys."

There was much in this varied tree growth to awaken Enda's interest. The fire scars, many large and deep, brought forth frequent questions. Occasionally after heavy wind storms, some decayed or less sturdy tree would fall upon its neighbors. If the trunk had been broken high enough for Enda to walk under the fallen tree, she always took occasion to route us that way. It seemed to appeal to her adventurous nature.

Keenly alive to the opportunities for varied adventure which her wilderness environment afforded, Enda was ever ready to start at any time in any direction, even though revisiting places she had seen recently and often. Her experimentation had taught her that there was always something new and different likely to turn up on every trip; she recognized the old familiar things with pleasure, and also she noticed any change along the way. More and more she appeared to be looking for the unusual, she liked variety, and had a constructive mind that was now quick to link cause and effect.

Enda was never allowed to have any fear of animals. Though she knew that our mountain wilderness was peopled with bear, lion, wild cat, coyote and skunk, there was always the accompanying idea that they did not harm people, unless they or their children were in danger or had been wounded. She always hoped we might see one of these attractions when we were out. She seemed to have established a firm conviction in her own mind that she would go and meet them if we did.

Coyotes especially stirred her imagination. She heard their calls, wondered what they meant, and frequently asked about their homes and how they lived. One spring she inquired why we had not heard any coyotes for so long. The explanation was that they had baby coyotes to watch and did not want to make it known where they were living. This gave her something more to think about, and she wanted to know what baby coyotes looked like, what they ate, and so forth.

Her father and I had talked of taking Enda and going to Timberline on Long's Peak. It was indeed an event to be put into the pack-sack the next morning, strapped to her father's back, and then to mount his horse Cricket with him. She was quiet as usual, giving alert attention to the adjustment of cinches and tying on our extra wraps, her special concern being given to the best place for the lunch.

Off we started at a lively canter, but not a murmur was heard from Enda about the unusual jostling. When we walked the horses up the first steep climb, she jumped up and down in the pack-sack to hasten our speed, and perhaps to assure us that there was no need of slowing up for her.

She often turned to see if I was enjoying the ride as much as she, but otherwise gave her undivided attention to all that we were passing. The first word was when a squirrel's chattering sounded from the distance. "Timmy" came out spontaneously. Through the merry aspen, the solemn spruce and fir we wound up the steep trail, commenting here and there, but mostly in silence. We stopped at the foaming cascades a few minutes to listen to its rush and roar, hoping to see a water ouzel. This gave the horses a chance to have a welcome drink.

When we arrived at Timberline Enda was taken out of the pack and waited nearby while we tied the horses. Enda was intent on every move we made. When I started to climb on one of the sturdy, long branched limber pine, she wanted to help me up. We took more pictures of trees and the views, then wandered off the rocky ridge to look for flowers. There were tiny forget-me-nots and yellow Potentilla less than an inch high, and masses of purple phlox and pink moss campion. Enda entered into our admiration of these, but did not linger, she did not want to miss anything.

The chipmunks seemed to surprise her, "Our chippie?" she asked. When told that these chipmunks lived up here all the time, she wanted to give them some of her lunch. We had a drink at the stream and again she wondered if this was the brook that passed our cabin.

When it came time to go home, Enda kept pointing to the saddle as though hoping she would be allowed to ride alone. So she was lifted upon Cricket for her picture and felt very proud indeed.

"Bye-bye flowers, bye-bye trees, bye-bye brook, bye-bye chippie," she called as we started down the trail. Much of the time she stood up in her pack on the back of the saddle to peer over her father's shoulder. At the places we had lingered on the way up, she pointed and indicated that we ought to stop and take pictures again. She called our attention to things she thought we might not see, the pale mid-day moon she exclaimed over as the "baby moon." She must have been a very tired little girl that night, for there was no coaxing her to bed. The whole day had been one of constant delight, if tiresome or fatiguing at any time for Enda, she gave no indication of it, apparently her enthusiasms prevented weariness.

The best school has perhaps been described as "The great outdoors with a child on one end of a log and a teacher on the other." Enda appears to have been one of the few registered in such a school.

The difficulty might be in keeping the child on the end of the log long enough to develop interest in anything. With Enda this was no effort, she seemed to be endowed with unusual capacities for enjoying life. Whatever the interest, at home or away visiting, she seized upon it with full enthusiasm. It was noticed that her outdoor interests never wore out, she was eager to hold down her end of the log. This might be explained that she felt our enthusiasm and was involved in the life we were living.

Children, through their intuitive sense, are quick to perceive the response to an environment and to life in general that is manifested by those with whom they live; but there is no sympathy for half-heartedness in anything.

It is my hope that with this biography other parents will make use of the freedoms of Nature, whose only certification as "teacher" is to be honestly interested in the individual child.

Enda on a pack trip with Warren Rutledge and Elizabeth Frayer Burnell, on their way to Hallett's Glacier. Circa 1928.

Esther Burnell Mills and Enda with Harold J. Cook on a hike.

PRIVATE OFFICE OF
WILLIAM T. HORNADAY
~~TWO MANHATTAN PARK BRIDGE, UNIVERSITY HEIGHTS~~
NEW YORK CITY

New York Zoological Park.
February 27, 1920

Mr. Enos A. Mills,
Longs Peak, Colo.

My dear Mr. Mills:

I thank you very much for a presentation copy containing your autograph of your beautiful new book "The Adventures of a Nature Guide." Surely this volume will be highly appreciated. I have found it very interesting and the illustrations bring the Rockies very near to the fireside.

I cordially endorse the idea of guides to nature, or nature guides. A good guide who knows the book of nature by heart makes a mountain trip about 400 per cent more interesting than it would be if taken without explanatory notes from a living teacher. Some men affect to despise guides, but I am not one of those. I dote upon them, and I hold that a poor guide is far better than none, and a good guide in an interesting country is a perpetual joy and well worth everything that they cost.

I never will forget the pleasure that I derived through being in the company of John M. Phillips, Charlie Smith and MackNorbos in the Canadian Rockies, and I am glad that a number of men have had opportunities to enjoy the company of that trio.

Wishing your book unbounded success, I remain,

Faithfully yours,

W. T. Hornaday

THE ROOSEVELT WILD LIFE
FOREST EXPERIMENT STATION

CHARLES C. ADAMS, DIRECTOR

SYRACUSE N. Y. June 22, 1921

Dear Mr. Mills:

Your note of the 14th was forwarded from New York where I am devoting some temporary editorial work on the College; but my permanent address is The Roosevelt Wild Life Forest Experiment Station, Syracuse N. Y.

I have not issued a book for some time — in fact I have been buying a good of my "Wild Life" — in fact I have been buying a good deal. I ship a bibliography from the Manual of the Audubon's Club. You ought to join us if you are not on that list in that way. Standards best. Ernest Thompson

Cordially, Ernest Thompson